D1003634

COUNT IT ALL JOY

COUNT IT ALL JOY

Reflections on Faith, Doubt, and Temptation
Seen Through the Letter of James

WILLIAM STRINGFELLOW

Wipf and Stock Publishers
EUGENE, OREGON

Wipf and Stock Publishers
199 West 8th Avenue, Suite 3
Eugene, Oregon 97401

Count It All Joy
By Stringfellow, William
Copyright©1967 Eerdmans
ISBN: 1-57910-291-3
Publication date: October, 1999 .
Previously published by Eerdman's Publishing Co., 1967.

For
Edward Kale

Acknowledgments

Some of the material here was first developed in lectures at the Ecumenical Study Conference of the United Christian Youth Movement, at a conference of Lutheran pastors in Minneapolis, at the College of Preachers at the Washington Cathedral. Some was introduced in addresses at San Francisco Theological Seminary, The College of Wooster, Harvard College, the Oklahoma Disciples of Christ Youth Convention, the Laymen's Conference of the Wisconsin Council of Churches, The Wayside Chapel in Sydney, Australia, and at an annual meeting of the Canadian Conference of Christians and Jews.

In various way preparation of the manuscript has been aided by William Eerdmans Jr., Mary Laschkewitzch, the Rev. Nicholas Holt and the Rev. T. D. Noffs.

Biblical quotations are from the Revised Standard Version.

The Revised Standard Version of the *Letter of James* is reprinted here as an aid and addendum, and is used by permission of the Division of Christian Education of the National Council of the Churches of Christ in the United States of America.

Count it all joy, my brethren, when you meet various trials, for you know that the testing of your faith produces steadfastness. And let steadfastness have its full effect, that you may be perfect and complete, lacking in nothing.

James 1:2-4

Contents

Introduction

These are harsh days for Protestants in America.

American Protestants suffer the pathetic anxieties of a people once ascendant and reigning, but now defensive and in retreat.

Protestantism is under fire from within and endures assault from without. A whole cadre of new critics — theologians, sociologists, and clergy (not to mention lawyers) — find the inherited denominational institutions worldly, self-serving, and decadent. Not only do the organized churches seem irrelevant to contemporary life, such critics argue, but the religion enshrined within them is dead. Other critics have gone further than condemning, as outmoded and ridiculous, acculturated ideas of God, and have proclaimed that God Himself is dead. In society outside the churches, meanwhile, a furious and fearfully complicated revolution is overturning the status quo in race, education, economics, and politics, a status quo that Protestantism had, in large measure, originated and sanctioned and by which, in return, Protestantism has been very extravagantly endowed.

These are days of terrific confusion for American Protestantism — for some Protestants they are even days of hysteria. While accepting substantial support from the state — in preferential tax treatment, in distribution of surplus food and medical supplies abroad, in federal assistance to church-related colleges, universities and hospitals — Protestants are at the same time still intoning the doctrine of separation of church and state. And, where the confusion becomes hysterical, while accepting such subsidies from the state, many Protestants belabor

11

the banning of prayer in public schools and fret over whether the name of God will much longer be inscribed on Caesar's coins.

These are days when the profound hypocrisy of American Protestantism is exposed for everybody, including the Protestants, to behold. That is most emphatically true in the racial crisis. After decades of platitudes and paternalism, some white Protestants have finally made a serious commitment to integration in American public life. Through their churches, some hundreds of thousands of dollars have even been volunteered to this cause. Yet, at the same time, Protestants both as individuals and as churches, with a handful of exceptions, have maintained and multiplied their enormous holdings in enterprises which condone racism in hiring, contracting, advertising, merchandising, promotions and the like. And, for all their own banalities, in the present social revolution the churches of American Protestantism that are revealed as the most vigorous, relevant and loving are the Negro churches.

On another front, these are poignant days for Protestants because the event least expected by so many Protestants has come to pass — the Roman Catholics, renewed by the witness of Pope John, have recognized Protestants as fellow Christians, have privileged them to be privy to the most authoritative deliberations within the Roman Church, and, on occasion, have publicly embraced Protestants. The ecumenicity maturing among the Romans is an acute embarrassment to those Protestants in America whose existence and identity has so much depended upon mere enmity for Rome.

These are harsh days for American Protestantism, but, nevertheless, they are also days of excitement and promise in which — through all the apprehension, consternation, double-mindedness and surprise, Protestants, along with other Christians, are beckoned to renewal in the faith and into maturity in Christ. These trials are to be accounted as joys.

In one respect more than in any other is the regeneration of Protestantism in the Christian faith most urgent and essential. It is in that which is the foundation for anything else worth salvaging in Protestantism. It is, as every Protestant must at least secretly suspect, in the return of the Protestants to the Word of God in the Bible.

Protestantism's Rejection of the Bible

The weirdest corruption of contemporary American Protestantism is its virtual abandonment of the Word of God in the Bible. That is ironic because access to the Bible and devotion to the Word of God in the Bible was that out of which authentic Protestantism came into being. It is strange, too, because, though the Bible suffers such neglect in Protestantism, the Protestants continue to boast of their esteem for the Bible. In one degree or fashion or another, this condition exists in all the churches of American Protestantism: the sects as well as the established denominations, the churches with ancestries in other countries and those indigenous to America.

The Bible has been closed in preaching in American congregations, for one thing, for a very long time. It has been my fortune to circulate widely among the churches of Protestantism in all parts of the nation and in all sectors of the confessional spectrum, in churches rich and poor, rural and urban, segregated and integrated, conservative and liberal, small and large. I can barely recall having heard in them Biblical preaching. Instead I have heard both dull and interesting opinions of clergy about religious etiquette, ecclesiastical politics, moral behavior and oddments, and all of this has been, where not actually heretical, typically inane, corny and preposterous. But very seldom is there the confident and responsible exposure of God's own Word in a manner in which the people may know and rejoice in the event of the Word of God and (to refute those who stupidly suppose that Biblical preaching has no contemporary significance) be so enlightened in the Biblical Word that they discern and celebrate that very Word present and militant in modern society.

Alas, it is not only in preaching that the Bible has been closed or else misused and manipulated, but also in the liturgical life of much of American Protestantism, especially among the denominations and sects indigenous to this country. Remember that whether it be simple or elaborate, formal or spontaneous, any corporate public worship is liturgical. Whatever the style or dignity of a particular liturgy, the most important element is that the liturgy be Biblical. It is Scriptural integrity where the liturgy is a theatricalization of the Word of God in the Bible — that is indispensable to corporate worship in public, not the disposition, personal faith or particular gifts of the clergy presiding or the sincerity, beliefs or interest of the people gathered. Where such be not the case, where the ordained ministers are left to determine how the people worship and whom or what they worship, it is quite likely that it will not be the Word of God in this world which is acknowledged and enjoyed in public worship but instead some word of men, or the person of the clergyman, or the sect or churchly tradition itself. Unless it be in structure and content, in shape and meaning, a portraiture of the Biblical Word, no liturgy can be either essentially Scriptural or truly contemporary.

Beyond preaching and liturgics, there is the accompanying dis-association of "Christian education" from the Word of God in the Bible. Protestant "Sunday Schools" are generally dependent upon the services of volunteer teachers whose conscientious spirit is not enough to overcome either incompetence or falsehood. They are furnished curriculum materials, in many of the denominations, which have slight authorization in the Gospel or, what is just as important, in the realities of actual life of student or teacher. To compound the ab-surdity, the time commonly allowed is so abbreviated that a Sunday School teacher is achieving a lot to learn the names of the students and show an ordinary human concern for them as persons. The Bible has been discarded in Sunday School in favor of baby-sitting, group dy-namics, religious gibberish, moralistic counselling, sectarian indoc-trination, romantic versions of church history, and stories *about* the Bible which are, more often than not, editorially biased, badly drafted, and unbiblical anyway. Such may have a place in the Boy Scouts or Demolay, but this is no way for Christians to nurture their offspring.

All the while, Protestants remain responsible for the dichotomy in education between the "secular" and the "religious." They have sent their children to public schools on weekdays to learn science, language, and the arts and deposited them in Sunday School on the other day of the week to be taught "religion." They have been un-mindful of the elementary insight of the Gospel that *all* knowledge given to men — in mathematics and morals, in history and culture, in the sciences and aesthetics — is embraced in the truth of the Word of

God. For Protestants to be accommodated to the separation of "secular" and "religious" education dishonors the ubiquity of the Word of God in this world and misleads the young into the notion that "religion" is something precious, pietistic, private and isolated from practical life. No particular commendation is bestowed here on parochial schools, after the manner of the Roman Catholics, since I know something of their compromises and corruptions, but it does seem to me irrefutable that the *idea* of parochial education is more sound and sensible than the juxtaposition of Sunday School and public school, so far as acquainting the young with the Biblical faith and its affirmation of all sorts of knowledge is concerned.

Protestants, of course, have been fiercely attentive to preserving a veneer of religiosity (*not* Christianity) in secular schools. Many Protestants who become frantic, as was mentioned, about the recital of so-called prayers and whether verses of the Bible are read (inevitably out of context) in classrooms, have never even considered praying with their own children at home nor have they become upset because the Bible is virtually banned in Sunday School. Protestants in America have been so much preoccupied in maintaining the public schools nominally religious that they have defaulted in establishing either their homes or churches as places of Christian teaching and learning.

Nowadays Protestants in America are neither intimate with nor reliant upon the Word of God in the Bible, whether in preaching, in services in the sanctuaries, or in education and nurture. Yet it is the Word of God in the Bible that all Christians are particularly called to hear, witness, trust, honor and love. It is only in that Word that Protestantism can have either vivacity or probity anymore.

Listening to the Word of God

I beg you not to be misled by my affirmation of the availability and centrality of the Word of God in the Bible, nor by my deploration of the diffidence toward the Bible in American Protestant preaching, liturgics, and teaching. As to the latter, I know that there are, here and there, notable exceptions to the allegations made; that there are such exceptions only sharpens the indictment. As to the former, let it be said bluntly that my esteem for the Word of God in the Bible does not mean that I am a Biblical literalist or a fundamentalist of any sort. Paradoxically, the trouble with fundamentalists, as I try to listen to them, is their shocking failure to regard and use the Bible conscientiously enough. If they honored the Bible more highly they would appreciate that the Word of God will endure demythologizing, that the Word cannot be threatened by anything whatever given to men to discover and know through any science or discipline of the world, or hindered by textual criticism, or hampered by linguistic analysis, or harmed by vernacular translations. All these are welcome to Christians as enhancements of the knowledge of the fullness of the Word of God and of the grandeur of men's access to the Word. More than that, if the fundamentalists actually took the Bible seriously they would *inevitably* love the world more readily, instead of fearing the world, because the Word of God is free and active in this world and Christians can only comprehend the Word out of their involvement in this world, as the Bible so redundantly testifies.

I am no Biblical scholar; I have neither competence nor temperament to be one. The ordinary Christian, layman or clergyman, does not need to be a scholar to have recourse to the Bible and, indeed, to live within the Word of God in the Bible in this world. What the ordinary Christian is called to do is to open the Bible and listen to the Word.

Listening is a rare happening among human beings. You cannot listen to the word another is speaking if you are preoccupied with your appearance or impressing the other, or if you are trying to decide what you are going to say when the other stops talking, or if you are debating about whether the word being spoken is true or relevant or agreeable. Such matters may have their place, but only after listening to the word as the word is being uttered. Listening, in other words, is a primitive act of love, in which a person gives himself to another's word, making himself accessible and vulnerable to that word.

It is very much like that when a man comes to the Bible. He must first of all listen to the Word which the Bible speaks, putting aside, for the time being, such other issues as whether the Word is credible or congenial or consistent or significant. By all means, if you will, raise these questions, but, first, *listen to the Word*.

Let the Bible be treated, too, with at least the respect you accord a letter from a person. If you receive a letter and care to know the word of the letter you would not open it, read a paragraph or two and then abandon it for two or three months, pick it up again to read a few more sentences on another page, leave it aside once more and later return to it again. No. If you care about the word of the letter, you would open it and listen to it attentively as a whole. After that, you might go back to this or that part of it to ponder or dispute, but first you would read it in its own context, asking only, What is being said? What is the word? The Bible deserves that much regard. And, if one cares to discern the Word of God in the Bible, then one must listen to the Bible in the Bible's own context and not deal with the Bible in a random, perfunctory, smattering fashion.

Some will think this a naïve approach to the Word of God in the Bible. I suppose it is just that. It is one which simply affirms that the Word of God has content, integrity and life which belongs to God Himself and that this can be received and comprehended by ordinary human beings. It is a view that regards the Bible more as a newspaper than as a systematic body of theological doctrine or as religious instruction or as moral law or, for that matter, as mere esoteric mythology. The Bible reports the news of the Word of God manifest and militant in the events of this history in a way that is accessible, lucid and edifying for the common reader. The Word of God is for men, and through the Bible that Word is addressed to men where they are, just as they are, in this world.

Such naïveté toward the Word of God does not repudiate or threaten other ways in which the Bible may be esteemed and used — as theology, mythology, poetry, literature, symbol, prophecy, ethics, or chronicle. But it does insist that any man may listen to the Word in the Bible innocent of any special skill or learning. And it does mean that all other uses of the Bible are subject to the discipline of God's own living Word as such and *not* the other way around, when men impose their own opinions, prides, methods and interpretations upon the Bible as if to test the Word of God by the words of men.

God speaks for Himself in this world, no man speaks in His stead; though, by God's grace, a man may hear God's Word and become a witness to it.

Interpreting the Bible

In the churches and outside the churches it is quite popular in the present day (though also, as the Letter to the Colossians indicates, in earlier times) to suggest that the content of the Word of God in the Bible is a matter of such indifference to God that it is only a question of the interpretations and insights of men. The unavoidable corollary is that one man's view is as apt as another's, which is, of course, a way of denying the integrity of the Word of God and, as the "death of God" vogue illustrates, ends in a denial of the existence of God.

A similar issue arises in the relationships of persons. This introduction is, for example, being written during a visit to Australia, during which I have met a great variety of people in a diversity of situations. In another two weeks, if the world lasts that much longer, and if I live, I will be back at work in New York encountering clients and colleagues there. If, somehow, all of those with whom I have been in this time, gathered together in the same room, they would each be able to speak of the one whom each has met in terms of the specific and various circumstances of each meeting. If I have integrity as a person, it will be discernible, as each one speaks of having somewhere and somehow met me, that each and every one testifies to having met the same person despite the diversity of conditions and locations of these happenings. Though the testimony of these many witnesses vary in many ways, it will nonetheless be evident that it is one person of whom they speak, who has been made known to them in different places and manifold circumstances. On the other hand, if, as a person, I have no integrity, if I am instead playing roles in these varying situations, if my own existence is a pretense and has no independence from the impressions or opinions of those whom I meet here and there, then it is as if I exist only in the interpretations of others; then it is as if I do not really exist at all.

The problem of the interpretations that men make of the Bible is similar. The Bible is a wondrously diversified testament of the Word of God disclosed to men in an array of events in which it is discernible that it is the same One of whom all these witnesses speak. God *is* and God possesses an existence and integrity of His own quite free from those who witness to Him or those who feign to do so. The versatility of God's witness to Himself in the Bible and continually in the world must not be used against God to try to prove that His Word is no more than what men interpret it to be. Rather this versatility of witness should provoke men to marvel at God's freedom and elusiveness from being captured by the intelligence, pietism, imagination or merit of men.

In other words, let all *religious* people beware. Their earnest longing for God is predicated on the reservation on their part that it is necessary for them to do something to find God. The Word of God in the Bible, however, is that God does not await human initiative of any sort but seeks and finds men where they are, wherever it be. No man can approach the Bible with any expectation of there discerning the integrity of the Word of God in such radical versatility if his mind is still obstructed or if his heart is still hardened by the notion that it is his task to locate or define God.

So, if I know who I am as a person and if I care to be known to another, it is a matter of my discretion that I make myself known to another. There is nothing that another can do about it, except to welcome or reject the gift, but neither of these affects my existence as such or the tender of knowledge of myself to the other. Similarly, insofar as God cares to be known of men, it is alone for Him to make Himself known, which, according to the manifold witness of the Bible, is exactly what He has done in this world.

To know the Word of God in the Bible, a man must come to the Bible with a certain naïveté, confessing that if God exists at all, He lives independently, though not in isolation, from any man's intelligence, longing, emotion, insight or interpretations, even those which divine the truth. He must be open to God's initiative. He must be bereft of all preconceptions. He must surrender all his own initiative. He must forego anything that would demean God to de-

pendence upon his thoughts, words, entreaties, deeds or moods. He
must take the appalling risk — by giving up all hypotheses, specula-
tions, ideas and deductions about God — that God is not and that
there is only death. When a man is so naked, so helpless, so transparent, when a man so utterly ceases to try to justify himself or anyone or anything else, he first becomes vulnerable to the Word of God,
which overcomes oblivion, heals deafness, restores sight and saves
men from manipulation, arrogance and folly in confronting the Word
of God in the Bible. When a man becomes that mature as a human
being he is freed to listen and at last to welcome the Word in the
Bible, and he is enlightened to discern the same Word of God at
work now in the world, in (of all places!) his own existence as well
as in (thank God!) all other life. Thus is established a rhythm in the
Christian's life encompassing his intimacy with the Word of God in
the Bible and his involvement with the same Word active in the world.

The Letter of James

The intention of this book is to affirm the urgency of immersion
in the Word of God in the Bible for the practice of the Christian life
in the world by approaching the Letter of James, asking, first of all,
what does it say? This book is not an attempt definitively to exegete
James, or to construct a technical commentary on the Letter. It is,
rather, a layman's reflection upon and exposition of some of the
themes of the first chapter of James. It is to be followed, after a while,
with further volumes which deal, in the same fashion, with issues in
the remainder of the Letter, such as the nature of good works, the
problem of riches, the economy of judgment, and the meaning of
vocation, patience for the eschaton, and the significance of love here
and now. This initial volume of the series deals with the knowledge
of God, doubt, and temptation.

James is, I know, a most neglected Letter: sometimes dismissed,
much maligned, often ignored, seldom used in the churches even in
fragments or for favorite verses. To some James will seem a re-
dundant Letter, to some as one containing contradictions. James is
controversial in its treatment of the tension between faith in God's

sufficient grace and the service of good works. The author seems to be so severe with the rich as to tempt the poor into self-righteousness. He seems at odds with some of the Letters of Saint Paul; Luther at one point all but discarded it (though he changed in this); many modern Christians have scarcely heard of it. These are precisely the reasons for turning to this Letter now. If it is little known, perhaps one can approach it free from preconceptions. Perchance that which is apparently contradictory expresses in fact the paradox of the Gospel reconciling opposites. Maybe that which tempts the poor is the same pride that James denounces among the rich. If this letter be controversial, that is a welcome relief in times when churches and churchmen are so beset with conformity to the world.

— WILLIAM STRINGFELLOW

Chapter One: *Wisdom*

Chapter One: WISDOM

> *If any of you lacks wisdom, let him ask God, who gives to all men generously and without reproaching, and it will be given him.*
>
> James 1:5

Wisdom means knowledge of God.

Wisdom is the knowledge of God given to men in this world which embraces all other knowledge within the limits of human awareness and comprehension, particularly the profound knowledge of self in relationship to all men and all things in this world.

Knowledge as Gift

The knowledge of God in which the truth of all existence inheres is an authentic gift and not something earned through diligence or piety, or rewarded for sacrifices of any description, or dependent upon any human initiative, or contingent upon the beliefs of men. It is a *gift,* and as with any genuine gift it originates wholly in the disposition of the donor and is accomplished entirely by the voluntary action of the donor. A gift can be refused or dishonored, one can vainly imagine himself deserving of a gift, a gift can be squandered or misconstrued, one may despise or be threatened by the generosity of the giver, but no responses such as these in any way negate the event of the gift, impair its value, or impeach the donor.

It is thus when one person makes a gift to another; it is no less so when a gift is made by God.

25

In American society, integrity in giving is rare. Giving has come to designate all sorts of transactions that bear little resemblance to gifts. People "give" out of a sense of obligation; they describe exchanges of chattels as "gifts"; they contribute to charities to purchase a sense of satisfaction; they "give" presents to one another in almost automatic reaction to commercial stimuli; they observe days and seasons with ritual "giving." Such vulgarities are no gifts. The real gift is always voluntary, spontaneous, free of expectancy either of equivalent return or gain of any kind, and representative of the giver. Actually the only thing that can be given by a person to another is himself. Any authentic gift is a means by which one offers to another knowledge of himself in a way that affirms the identity of the recipient as well as declares who the donor is. A gift is a sacrament of existence in a relationship established by the initiative of the giver. The prerogative in the relationship belongs wholly to the act of giving. No one can really know me unless I give him such knowledge. I can not truly know another unless he gives that knowledge to me.

The wisdom that constitutes knowledge of God and within that, all knowledge, is verily a gift, given to men by God in this world. Jesus Christ is the epitome of that gift. This does not mean that men in this world are bereft of knowledge of God apart from Christ, for knowledge of God is given in all created things; rather, it means that all that is known of God in this world is embraced, verified and consummated in Jesus Christ. In Jesus Christ all that men may know in this world of God is made known. It is not beyond God's mercy that there is more to know of Him than that given to men in this world to know, but it is the measure of God's love for this world that no more is known of Him than that which is known through Jesus Christ.

God is neither shy nor modest in giving knowledge of Himself to men, for this gift is given to all men whether a man welcomes or ignores it. From no man is this gift withheld despite even the power of sin. The gift is offered in the first instance, as it were, in the event of Creation itself; but the gift is renewed in the Fall. No matter how terrible the emptiness men endure within themselves and the alienation men suffer from all other men and all things in their estrangement from God, that does not blot out the gift. Or, to put it in the images of Genesis, after the Fall, in the depths of man's emphatic rejection of God and pathetic negation of man's own life, the first characterization of God's response to rejection is of God walking in the garden calling to man "Where are you?" (Genesis 3:8-9). In sin men hide from God and conceal themselves from one another and fear even to behold themselves; but, in the midst of that, God is seeking men.

That God's love is indomitable, that God perseveres in being available to men, that God reaches out to men though they be sinners, that God's gift of Himself transcends all barriers, attempts to escape, or temptations — all this means that just as God's authorship includes the whole of Creation so also He wills that all of Creation be restored and that all men be saved as His gift. The knowledge of God which is salvation is a gift for *all* men, though every man may not accept the gift and though churchly doctrines may try to hamstring God's grace with religious indulgences. God gives generously and without reproaching (James 1:5b).

Knowledge of God and Religion

But if wisdom is the knowledge of God as a gift and if Jesus Christ epitomizes that gift, what is to be thought of the historic religions of men? Are they to be dismissed because they do not so regard and honor Christ? Are they to be suppressed as enemies of the Gospel? Are their adherents to be proselytized because they are pagans or are they to be shunned as unbelievers? Or, as some would have it, is the Christian faith essentially undistinguished from the religions? Is some common element to be found both in the Gospel and in the religions that diminishes the importance of any differences between them? And what of all the other varieties of religious belief and commitment common to men — the personal conceptions, notions, motivations and, sometimes, superstitions, even hallucinations — which constitute the actual faith of many persons? Is there some kind of equality among the hosts of religions, both the great and popular ones and those merely individualistic, and the ancient ones as well as those which survive today, which means that one religion is as valid or efficacious as another? Is religion anyway such a private affair that inquiry into the comparative claims of the various faiths is precluded? Is it arrogance that underlies the much repeated assertion of Christians that there is something unique about their faith that sets it apart from all other faiths?

As the term is intended here, religion is an art in which men contemplate and inquire into the nature of ultimate reality and in which, through speculation, reflection, meditation and discipline, men conceptualize and, more or less, systematically formulate their convictions so derived. Further, it is an attempt to prove or defend the truth and efficiency of their views, to discern and try to apply the implications of these views to personal existence and the life of the world insofar as there may be such implications, and invent, institute and practice rituals and observances that express their allegiance to the conception of ultimate reality that they have made, found, inherited or otherwise accepted.

Religion, thus, is a human enterprise presupposing the existence of some god or gods or principle or force or object which has moral significance in some way for men in this world, whether that be fear of punishment, purpose, a promise of immortality, a claim of righteousness, assurance of happiness or whatnot. Religion claims significant insight into those characteristics of the existence of ultimate reality, however defined or conceived, which provide guidance for men in seeking and establishing relationships with that existence. What is known in this world of ultimate reality or god consists of what men have discovered, learned, surmised, deduced or guessed from their own intellectual, emotional, physical and spiritual efforts.

There are very great qualitative differences between the formal and institutionalized religions of mankind, past and present, and the little, private religions with which some men satisfy themselves. The content of the former varies substantially in comparison one with the others, and the content of the latter varies with each religionist. On top of that, in each of the historic religions sects and factions abound with their peculiar interpretations of doctrine, distinctive ritual practices, and separate pietistic exercises. Yet for all such variances, all these forms of religion hold a common methodology; all share in the same essential approach to the religious issue. All consider religion as the human quest for God. All have confidence in the capacity of men, or, at least, of some men, to breach the mystery of God. All emphasize human initiative in establishing relationship with divinity. All focus upon some conception of God as the object of devotion, the source of meaning, and the determination of moral behavior.

It is exactly at this point — not necessarily in content, but in method — that the Christian Gospel is radically distinguished from all religions. The theme of the Gospel from the first moment of the Fall, as has been cited, is God in search of man. The emphasis is upon the initiative God takes toward men in the world. God volunteers relationship with men. God gives Himself for all mankind. What men may know of God is only that which God Himself discloses for men to know.

Thus the confession of faith characteristic of Christians, since the times of the Apostolic and Nicene Creeds, does not propound any idea or conception of God, but bespeaks, just as the Bible does, God's living presence and action in the world. The religions aspire to describe the attributes of God; the Gospel proclaims God's accomplishment in this world in meeting men where they are. It is upon this difference between the religions and the Christian faith that any responsible claim of uniqueness for Christianity rests, and not, as the people of the churches have so often and so fondly supposed, because God prefers Christians to other men.

What is distinguishable between some religion's conception of God and the Gospel of Christ can be seen analogically in human encounters. If you and I have never met, I may be nevertheless persuaded of your existence because I have heard others mention your name, or describe how you look, or report something that they claim you have said. I may read something that purports to be either by or about you. I may see a photograph that is said to be of you. There may be certain evidences of work that is attributed to you. I may meet someone who asserts that he has met you. From this and similar data I may conclude that you do exist and may go further and construct in my imagination an idea of what you are like; I can make for myself a concept of you. But then if the day comes to pass that I meet you I learn by my own sensibilities of your actual appearance that you do exist, that you look like you look and say what you say and act as you act. As persuaded of your existence and attributes as I might have been from my conception of you based upon data that had come to my attention before you confronted me in the flesh, I could never know for sure either whether you are or who you are without meeting you. But being met by you confirms both your existence and identity as such and establishes a relationship between us. In our meeting the conception that I had of you becomes obsolete. Knowing you, now, I no longer have need to suppose who you are. It may be, of course, of some routine and academic interest to me (and to you) how far my idea of you corresponds to the living person. My concept of you may turn out to be essentially or substantially true or it may have little or no similarity to you as you actually are. So be it. I am now no longer limited to my own conception of you, since we have in fact met, and I know that you *are* by that event and I know *who* you are in that which you have yourself given to me to know of who you are.

My conception of you, whether true or false, in any degree, is *not* you. In religion, a conception of God, whether true or false, in any degree, is *not* God. Upon this very issue, religion is superseded by the Gospel. In this way, all religions of men of whatever sort in whatever circumstances are fulfilled in the Gospel. On this count, the Gospel cannot even be classified as a religion. What dignifies any religion, even the false and idolatrous, is an inherent apologetic for the existence of God, somehow or other defined; what is bold in any religion, including those vain superstitions, is the ambition to explain God; what is audacious in Christian faith is the enjoyment of God's presence here and now, whatever the circumstances; what is radical about the Gospel is the news that religion can be now discarded, by virtue of God's grace.

Truth in Religion

Yet if the Gospel emancipates men from their religions, that does not mean that Christians can lightly discount the religions of

men. The disjuncture between the Gospel of Christ and the many
religions does not assume or require that the conceptions of God,
whatever they may be, in any religion may be rejected by Christians
arbitrarily or that they be ridiculed, demeaned or regarded as threatening to the Gospel.

In a given instance, the idea of God in a religion may be true or
may apprehend the truth in a significant way. Such perception is to
be welcomed, for it invites Christians to witness to God's presence in
all human endeavors, including religious enterprises, and it prays for
the very relief from the search for God that is the condition precedent
to Christian faith. Such insight is not to be dismissed by Christians
but upheld by them in a way that points beyond the insight to the
maturity of all that is true in Christ. More than that, *all* religious ideas,
whether true or false in terms of the Gospel, represent the aspirations
of men for the Gospel, and Christians are called to affirm such aspirations in their proclamation of the faith. Saint Paul furnished the
example when he visited the Athenians, beheld their longing for God
and for themselves, loved them for this, stood in their midst, and said:

> Men of Athens, I perceive that in every way you are very
> religious. For as I passed along, and observed the objects of
> your worship, I found also an altar with this inscription, "To
> an unknown god." What therefore you worship as unknown,
> this I proclaim to you. The God who made the world and every-
> thing in it, being Lord of heaven and earth, does not live in
> shrines made by man (Acts 17:22b-24).

The ground of the aspiration of men for the Gospel, whether
evidenced by religious ideas that are true or false, is the presence of
the Word of God in the existence of every man. It is this to which
the Christian appeals in proclamation, thus exposing and undoing
the distortion of the Word of God that all religious ideas represent
(cf. James 1:18; 1:21).

Much the same thing can be said of secular ideologies that
command the loyalties and service of men in a way that amounts to
religious commitment. The totalitarian ideologies are, of course,

examples of that, but so are Greek philosophy, humanism, utilitarian-
ism, and the legion of other philosophies and ideologies. However
they may be regarded under the judgment of the Word of God,
however Christians look upon them in the light of the Gospel, Christians recognize that they bespeak a hope for salvation and seek a
means of justification that can only be, and only is perfected, in
Jesus Christ.

Though the aspiration for the truth of the Word of God be
hidden within any and, in a sense, every religion or philosophy, this
does not make any of them less an indulgence or less idolatrous,
be they ever so sincere, benignly motivated or humane. The man
whose real object of worship is an idea of God or concept of good
that is of his own invention or to which he has been somehow persuaded, indulges in the flesh just as much as do gluttons or profligates.
And no matter how proximate any such propositions may be to the
truth of the Word of God, they are and remain idols just as much
as any graven image. God is not enshrined in the tabernacles of
human ideas or ideals, and it is vain for men to worship in such
precincts.

Thus the Christian witness *vis-à-vis* the religions of men, including the secular equivalents of religion in ideology and philosophy, is
dialectic: both the profundity and the futility of men's aspirations to
save themselves are exposed in one and the same proclamation of the
Word of God.

The unique character of the Christian faith, as distinguished
from the religions, in a methodological sense, is reflected in the
practice of the Christian life as contrasted with the practice of religion.
It is, as it were, that the principle of sacrifice common to religion of
all sorts is turned upside down in the Christian faith. In religion
sacrifices in one form or another must be offered to establish relationship with the deity and to please or appease the deity. A fatted calf
must be slain and placed upon the altar, fasting or peculiar diets
or similar pietistic regulations must be observed by the religious,
certain moral behavior is prescribed, conformity of belief is required.
All these and similar ritualistic, moralistic or dogmatic exercises are

the specific forms of sacrifices made to the idea or image that takes the place of God.

In the Gospel, however, the principle of sacrifice is, so to speak, reversed. The emphasis there is upon the sacrificial gift God makes of His own life for all men. To be fastidious about it, there is really no such thing as a martyr in the Christian faith, for the true sacrifice has been made in behalf of men by God and it is His sacrifice that saves the world; to His sacrifice nothing whatever can be added by any man and by His sacrifice are all men freed from making any sacrifices. The man who has died in Christ, lives in Christ and if that man now is killed because he is a Christian, though he dies, he lives in Christ and his death is no sacrifice for him.

Christians are freed from making sacrifices in the manner that the religious do, but the offering of worship is made by them to God, both privately and publicly. Though in practice in the churches worship has been profaned and has become imitative of religious sacrifices, Christian worship that has integrity is never a particular offering of possessions, conduct or other tribute considered pleasing and acceptable to God; it is always the offering of all that one is, that which seems good or of which one is proud as well as that which does not seem good or of which one is ashamed. The Christian offers himself, his whole self, as both part and symbol of the Church's consecration of the whole world to God, knowing that no one and nothing so offered in worship is acceptable to God in and of itself. Yet this unacceptable offering is rendered worthy by God's acceptance of it. The Christian offering, far from resembling religious sacrifices, is the offering of one's self as a sinner and as a representative of all other men as sinners in confidence in the mercy of God's sufficient sacrifice for all men. For *all* men: that part of it is very important in distinguishing Christian worship from religious sacrifices. If, as the religious suppose, certain sacrifices can and must be made to secure divine approval and favor, then salvation extends only to those who have the stamina, wit or opportunity to make the prescribed sacrifices. The weak, uninformed, or absent are doomed. If God is fond of fatted calves, what shall become of those who keep none? If God is concerned only with those who recite precise religious formularies, what shall happen to the ignorant? If salvation depends upon correctly second-guessing God's judgment of each decision and action, then all of mankind will certainly suffer damnation.

God has shown men a more excellent way than religion. In His gift of Himself, in His sacrifice of His life, all religions have been transcended, hence all human sacrifices can be abandoned. He has made Himself known to men and so the foolishness of religion is undone in the wisdom that is the gift of knowledge of Him (cf. James 3:13-18).

The Religions and the Biblical Faiths

A question remains whether that which distinguishes Christianity from the religions does not just as much distinguish Judaism from the religions. Are not both the great Biblical faiths set apart from the religions since both witness to God's initiative in disclosing Himself in history in a redemptive way?

The issue of the relation of Christians and Jews is beclouded by the vitality of syncretism in American society. The necessities of pluralism in race, religion and national origin are thought by many Americans to require the minimization of differences and, on occasion, to justify the suppression of differences. In the realm of faith the tradition has grown that while individuals may have their own preferences, the public discussion of the varieties of belief is divisive and should be avoided in favor of emphasis upon what all faiths are asserted to share in common. This is, so far as both the Biblical faiths are concerned, a form of secularization, and it issues in the idea that the single most important thing is the mere profession of belief itself. (Americans are great believers in believing.) To inquire beyond that is to become too personal and, more important, is likely to expose disagreements and risk divisions in society. If anything is to be ventured let it be only into those so-called moral and spiritual values—like the golden rule—to which all are assumed to give assent.

Neither Christians nor Jews can conscientiously accommodate themselves to such syncretistic notions as these, though in fact multitudes of both Jews and Christians (especially Protestants) in America have done just that. Faith in faith itself ranks, from a Biblical point of view, as superstition; to affirm the action of God in human history, as both Jews and Christians do, means that faith is not merely or essentially a personal matter but on the contrary profoundly political and social. Neither Jews nor Christians can give assent to handy maxims like the golden rule (that is, if the golden rule means, as it is commonly interpreted, either enlightened self-interest or prudent reciprocity in dealings with one another). Such maxims hardly express the gist of either Judaism or the Gospel.

That neither Christians nor Jews can become syncretists without denouncing their Biblical inheritances does not, however, dispose of the question whether the distinction between the religions and the Christian faith applies as well to the religions and Judaism. That issue is now further dramatized by the maturing of the ecumenical movement.

Judaism and Ecumenism

Reunion of the Church organically is the vocation of the ecumenical movement. The Church, of course, has suffered organic disunity for a very long time: from the early days of the Apostolic Church, in fact, through the schisms between East and West, in the Reformation and its aftermaths, to the modern era in which a radically debilitating denominationalism was proliferated in the United States and then exported elsewhere in the world where missionaries from this continent colonized. Organic reunion of the Church in a way that transcends such brokenness and restores the integrity of the Church's oneness at Pentecost, when the Church was given to the world by God, is no mere cause of the Church, however. Reunion of the Church of Christ is the *world's* most urgent and pathetic need. It is *that* because the unity and wholeness of the Church is the pioneer and ambassador of the reconciliation of the whole world. The Church of Christ exists for *no* other reason than to show within the Church's own life as a community in the world how God's grace overcomes all human barriers, forgives all alienations, heals all brokenness, absolves all distinctions, pacifies all strife, purifies all iniquity, sanctifies the vulgar, redeems from sin and defeats the last enemy, which is death. The Church is established in the world and is given to the world only for the sake of mission, only as a witness, only to be the forerunner of the world reconciled. That mission is retarded or spoiled when the Church is divided by anything which divides the world. That purpose and task is thwarted and crippled when the churches, thus divided, become devoted to nation or race or class or privilege or property or any other thing by which men are separated from one another in this world. That service is corrupted and compromised where the Church condones organic disunity (let it be admitted that most American Protestants do so condone disunity), or when the Church becomes consecrated to its own existence in disunity or in other forms of worldliness.

The ecumenical movement has nothing at all to do with the creation of some "super-church" or with the mere institutional reorganization of the existent churches. It is not even essentially about reaching a concord of faith, for that has already been given in Jesus Christ, and that is not something the Church achieves or makes but is something either accepted or repudiated. Fundamentally, the ecumenical movement is about how the Church serves the world by the precedent of unity for the reconciliation of the world.

That everyone everywhere is therefore beneficiary of the ecumenical movement (whether he appreciates it or not), that all nations and institutions are vested with an interest in ecumenical negotiations (whether they realize it or not), that the ecumenical task has been delivered into the custody of the Church only for the sake of the world (whether the churches welcome or honor such a trust or not) poses the issue of the relations between Christians and Jews and between both of them and the various religions in an acute form.

According to Biblical tradition — though contrary to the tradition of the religions — the Jews are chosen by God as an exemplary people, as His own nation, as His priest among the nations (cf. Hebrews 11:1-40). But the election of the Jews does not constitute their own salvation only; it consists of their witness as the pioneers of the salvation of all mankind. The Jews are called to *ecumenical* vocation. It is precisely to this task of ecumenical mission in the world to which the Church claims succession. It is this witness that Christians claim to inherit from the Jews. It is this mission to which the churches turn and return through the ecumenical movement. In this respect the Christians are now the true Jews. For the world, the Church is now Israel. The vocation that the old Israel knew is now, by the virtue of God's patience, the task of the Church of Christ.

If the comity of American pluralism opposes recognition of the continuity of the ancient ecumenical calling of the Jews and the contemporary ecumenical office of the Christians, then Christians will simply have to suffer that opposition. In any case, the convenience of pluralistic ethics excuses neither Christians nor Jews from acknowledging that what essentially distinguishes both from the various religions is the witness in all the world to the saving acts of God in history.

At the same time neither Christians nor Jews honor their respective faiths if they fear or flinch at confronting the fact that it is the claim to ecumenical authority in the world which divides them from one another. There is, after all, a momentous distinction between Judaism and Christianity that neither can ignore and still retain integrity. There *is* a difference between the faith of the Old Testament bereft of the New Testament, and the Old Testament, as it were, encompassed in the confession of the New Testament. At the heart of the difference is the issue of whether the acts of God in this history for salvation are both culminated and consummated in Jesus Christ. The Jews believe no such thing; the Christians believe exactly that.

Some Christians and some Jews, as well as many Americans of neither faith, recoil at putting the difference between Judaism and Christianity so starkly, even though since the establishment of the Christian Church at Pentecost the singular issue between Judaism and Christianity has been, simply, *Jesus Christ*. Who is He? What does His coming among men mean? How shall He be received? Why is He on the Cross instead of that insurrectionist? Was He truly raised from death? Does He reign in history? Is He the One who is Judge of all? Who *is* Jesus Christ?

Humanists within the Jewish community and within the Christian Church and secular humanists all urge that such questions be put aside lest they upset relations between Jews and Christians, cause what the two great Biblical faiths share in common to be lost sight of, and inhibit practical collaboration between the two in American society. The humanists would thus seduce both Jews and Christians into a compromise that would vitiate the faith of each. It is, on the contrary, only when there is candid dialogue between Jews and Christians about what fundamentally distinguishes them from each other that there can be mutual respect and, indeed, love between the two. It is in recognition of the momentous difference between Judaism and Christianity that Jews and Christians can cherish their common inheritance in the Old Testament. It is only when that which divides Jews and Christians is openly articulated that each can be bold enough to trust the other in concerted action in practical issues in society.

It is one of the fruits of the deep secularization of Judaism and the radical sectarianism of Christianity in America that intolerance is imputed to recognition and discussion of the difference between the two. Rather the opposite should be done: the man who speaks from his conscience as a Jew is bound to show his reverence for the humanity of others; the Christian who confesses the Gospel by that gesture evidences his love for others. The *real* intolerance possesses those who, in the name of tolerance, would suppress men of faith by forbidding the open proclamation of what they believe, why they so believe, and how they differ. The true bigots, in America at least, are those who, believing in nothing beyond themselves, insist that everyone else follow suit, intimidating into silence anyone who, as Jews and Christians do, believes in more than himself and dares to say so publicly.

But if there is some residue of freedom in this country to practice candor in matters of faith (about which I have an increasing doubt), as in the issue between Judaism and Christianity, then, as a Christian, I am constrained to say that, though Israel received the wisdom that is knowledge of the living God, which cannot be eradicated even if renounced, and though God elected the Jews as His people, which can never be revoked even if disclaimed, Israel grew skeptical of the wisdom delivered unto her and became suspicious of God's abundance of grace as the prophets have told.

When the day came to pass that Israel was confronted with the fulfillment and fullness of wisdom in Jesus Christ, when the day came to pass that Israel beheld in Jesus Christ the grandeur and scope of God's election, Israel's skepticism and suspicion triumphed over her faith. Israel rejected Christ and thus abdicated her election to the ecumenical mission.

Thereafter Israel suffers the radical separation of faith from ethics. Revelation, the gift of wisdom, is crowded out by ritualistic observance, moralism and ecclesiastical authoritarianism. In other words, in the repudiation of Christ, Israel chooses to become a facsimile of religion, though Israel remains still and forever set apart from the religions by the irrevocable nature of God's favor in first choosing the Jews as His own people in the world.

Anti-Semitism and the Crucifixion

A word had better be said right here, however, about anti-Semitism, especially as it survives in America among professing Christians. Anti-Semitism is still prevalent in the United States, though it is not a matter of national policy, as it was in Nazi Germany, and it is not as bestial as it was in the Nazi era. It has not disappeared from American life, either because the Jews have become as assimilated as many of them have in this country and culture, or because so many of them are victims of secularization. Surely among the causes of anti-Semitism in America has been the profound prejudice among white Anglo-Saxon settlers and their heirs, who for so long dominated American politics and the American economy, against all ethnic, national and religious origins different from their own. Though many immigrant groups have been assimilated substantially into American society, few who have immigrated to this country have been spared discrimination upon their arrival here and the residue of this sort of prejudice still survives. Yet the Jews have suffered more than the usual discrimination against immigrants. For a very long time, let it be confessed, anti-Semitism has been one of the status marks of the white Anglo-Saxon Protestant middle and upper classes, evidenced by the exclusion of Jews from certain professions, clubs, residential areas, political recognition and the like.

I make no pretense of understanding anti-Semitism in America in such forms as these beyond suggesting that it is not at all sufficiently explained in terms of the traditional bias experienced and usual barriers encountered by immigrant peoples and that it is partially explained in attitudes towards the Jews inherited by Christians of all sorts in this nation, as well as elsewhere in the world. Whatever else may be said of anti-Semitism and its causes, it must be acknowledged that anti-Semitism has had substantial roots in the churches and in the views propagated in the churches for so long about the Crucifixion of Christ.

I refer, obviously, to the notion — *utterly without support in the Bible* — widely believed by multitudes of church members that the Jews are solely or, at least, especially, responsible for the Crucifixion both at the time of the actual event and also in the present day.

This matter, of course, has achieved unusual attention because of the controversy in the Vatican Council II about the schema on the Jews. As recently as September of 1964, however, after it was known that a schema was under consideration in the Vatican Council, a survey conducted by The Anti-Defamation League of B'nai B'rith indicated that 61 percent of the Catholics in America believed the Jews to be responsible for crucifying Christ, while only 22 percent fixed the responsibility on the Romans of the time. The same survey showed that fundamentalist Protestants were even more hostile to the Jews than Catholics. Subsequently the Episcopal House of Bishops became the first major ecclesiastical authority in the United States to declare that the Jews were not guilty of Christ's Crucifixion, although, unhappily, as the matter was widely reported in the media and, I fear, understood by the public, the implication was that the Christians had just finally come around to granting the Jews amnesty, whereas, in fact, the declaration exonerates the Jews from guilt in the first instance.

Meanwhile, in the Roman Church the matter became embroiled not only in the contention for power between so-called liberal and

conservatives among the Fathers of the Roman Church but also in
the politics of the Arab-Israeli conflict.

One hopes that such controversy will help to free some Christians
from anti-Semitism, but one begins to despair that a forthright and
theologically responsible clarification will be made of the issue by any
duly constituted ecclesiastical authority.

The involvement of the Jews in the Crucifixion is not something
appropriately resolved as an issue of churchly politics or as one of
international politics. The question, theologically, is not whether all
Jews to the present day bear responsibility for the Crucifixion, and it
is not that some Jews long ago bear guilt for it. The issue is not
pardon, nor is it that no Jews are responsible. The issue is not *even*
exoneration. What needs to be affirmed and promulgated, if anti-
Semitism is to be exorcised from the churches is that, in truth, all
mankind throughout all time bears the guilt for the Crucifixion.

In truth, *all* mankind, including those at the very time who con-
spired and accused Jesus and those who betrayed and denied Him and
those who were privy to the trial and condemnation and those who
fixed Him to the Cross and those who beheld Him dying there, but,
as well, those who both preceded and all of us who have come after
these events, share the responsibility for the Crucifixion. *All mankind
is guilty*. The position of the Jews in the Crucifixion is, indeed, an
eminent one — not because they bear a greater, more particular or
unique guilt, but because they remain, even in the drama of the Crucifixion, God's chosen people, the representatives and ambassadors of
all mankind throughout all time before God. Thus, no man, whether
he be Jew or Roman, Christian or pagan, whether he lived in Biblical
times or lives today, no man at all escapes innocently from the shadow
of the Cross. No man is unimplicated in consigning Christ to the
suffering of death. No man has ever lived or ever will who does not
try to kill God.

Yet as all men are guilty in the deliverance of Christ to death,
so also are all become beneficiaries of Christ's triumph over death and
of the forgiveness that Christ besought for all men from the Cross.

Ecumenism and Evangelism

The Church succeeds Israel in the ecumenical mission in the world, but the authority of the Christian people as the new Israel is now subverted by the divisions of the Church into a multiplicity of sects and denominations.

The radical sectarianism of the American churches, in fact, is the most profound form of secularization that the Church suffers in contemporary life. Those divisions of the Church originating in property, language, race, locality or incidents of secular history (like the Civil War, the conquest of the frontier, the development of suburbia) institutionalize the repudiation of the unity of the Church at Pentecost, which transcends all such worldly distinctions. Those divisions of the Church attributable to obsessive regard for one or another of the manifold charismatic gifts, which are bestowed at Pentecost upon the Church only for the benefit of the world, scandalize the holiness and oneness of the Church's ministry in the world. Though God's witness to Himself in the world is not thereby estopped or even hindered, such disunity and such disorientation embodied in the inherited churchly institutions categorically, and pathetically, immobilizes the witness of the Church in the world.

By dishonoring the unity of the Church in Pentecost, the churches disown the ecumenical mission, and thus imitate the very apostasy of Israel: faith is isolated from ethics, worship becomes superstitious ritualism, dogma is supposed to have intrinsic efficacy, indulgences are sold, pietism corrupts freedom, the sanctuary becomes a refuge from the world, heresy is notarized, ecclesiastical status takes precedence over servanthood, ideological and sectional interests are confused with the Gospel, the young are deceived, strangers are unwelcome, God is treated as object rather than subject, the world is abandoned to death. The Christian faith takes on the façade of mere religion.

Where the ecumenical task is forsaken and the world is thereby renounced, evangelism can have little credibility. That is why so much of what goes on under the rubric of evangelism in the divided churches nowadays is *not* evangelism. There is, instead, proselytizing. It is not evangelism to induce people to join some church out of fear or the promise of favor. There is revivalism, too, some of it honest and some of it racketeer, but that only has integrity where it beseeches the organic reunion of the Church and addresses the needs of the world, not where it is aimed at reinforcing denominational fanaticism. There is much verbalization and pedantic argument, but words remain the most superficial way of communication and are hollow unless verified in action. There are many secular social pressures that inspire church affiliations and that is one reason why so many laymen, and not a few clergy, do not profess to be Christians and feel secretly guilty about it.

In the era of Christian disunity, all sorts of importunities and manipulations, schemes and gimmicks, deceptions and excuses have been passed off as evangelism. But the fact remains, despite either bona fide or corrupt intentions on the part of either the "evangelists" or the "evangelized" that so long as the Church is characterized, as the Church is today, by the secularization of sectarianism, what is called evangelism is bound to be perverted and authentic evangelism is certain to be scarce.

Evangelism, after all, in the Gospel of Christ, means the affirmation of the Word of God in the life of each and every human being in relation to all of creation. Evangelism, in the Gospel, is an enthusiastic expression of the love that Christ bears for the whole of the world, which is authorized by the experience of that same love which the evangelist has himself suffered.

The emasculation of the Church's evangelistic work, due to the organic disunity of the Church, has particular poignancy in the practical relationships of Christians and Jews. *So similar, indeed, is the apostasy of divided Christendom in the present day to that of the old Israel that I must argue that contemporary Christians are without authority to address the Jews evangelistically.*

By precisely the same token, and for the sake of the recovery of the ecumenical discipline of the Church as the successor of the old Israel, I am now persuaded that in *every* conversation, council, conference or comparable event in which various Christians of the several churches convene to examine the nature of the Church and the ecumenical mission in the world, the presence of the Jews is indispensable.

In other words, the original disposition of the Jews with respect to Christ, and, thus, toward the essential mission of Israel in the world is so like the present estate of the churches that call upon Christ's name, that professing Christians cannot afford the absence of the venerable insight of the Jews as to that knowledge of God given to men in this world in which the knowledge of all things inheres.

The ecumenical encounter — which is only about the organic reunion of the Church because it is about the restoration of organic unity to the world — must become focused in the dialogue of Christians and Jews.

Chapter Two: *Doubt*

Chapter Two: DOUBT

> *But let him ask in faith, with no doubting, for he who*
> *doubts is like a wave of the sea that is driven and tossed*
> *by the wind. For that person must not suppose that a*
> *double-minded man, unstable in all his ways, will*
> *receive anything from the Lord.*
>
> James 1:6-8

The knowledge of God in which faith is established is a gift of God to men in this world: a matter of God's election, not of human choice; the fruit of God's generosity, not a reward for the diligence of men; the sign of God's unconditional love for the world, not contingent upon human enterprise. Faith is a charismatic gift (cf. Ephesians 4:11-14; 3:5). Faith is the success of God's quest for men, not the outcome of men's search for God.

What does it mean, however, to ask God for the wisdom that is knowledge of Him and of one's own self in relation to all others and all things? How is such asking God for wisdom to be distinguished from any of the ways in which the religious search for God? How can a man, lacking wisdom, "ask in faith, with no doubting," as the Letter of James puts it? What does it mean to ask *in* faith *for* faith?

Asking in Faith for Faith

To ask God in faith for the knowledge of Him that embraces the profound knowledge of self in relation to the rest of creation is to enter upon an estate of utter helplessness. *Utter* helplessness: it is an

47

experience in which all is given up, in which all effort and activity of
whatever sort ceases, not only in which all answers are unknown, but
unattempted, and also in which all questions are inarticulated and
abandoned. It is a condition in which, as it were, a man stands totally
alone in the world — naked, bereft, transparent, immobile, absolutely
vulnerable in each and every facet of his person. It is the event in
which the alienation and brokenness of all relationships, including
a man's relationship with himslf, is actualized within a man's own
self. It is the existential realization of fallenness. It is the time in
the wilderness. It is the crisis of that unqualified helplessness which
is death.

This death is not the same thing as despair. The man who suffers
despair worships death as an idol in place of God; he is not yet *utterly*
helpless. His idolatry of death as the ultimate and immediate reality
of existence is the means by which he seeks to justify himself. Despair,
in this sense, is a perverted kind of hope. The man in despair may be
pathetic, but he has not yet acknowledged the futility of his search
for meaning though the religious quest has brought him to the point
of regarding death as god. He is still protesting, in his idolatry of
death, that he is not helpless.

I have never attempted suicide. I do not recollect ever seriously
contemplating suicide. I have known a number of persons who have
committed suicide, including a number of clients (though I trust
that is not a specific reflection on me as a lawyer). I suppose that the
most blunt example of a person whose despair amounts to the worship
of death as an idol is the person on the verge of suicide. He has,
it seems, left everything behind, forsaken his family, quit his job,
fled from friends, renounced the ordinary obligations of daily life,
abandoned his possessions. Everything appears now for him to be
reduced to one final decision — whether or not to take his own life.
Though he be in panic, he has not in fact surrendered all hope of
finding meaning in existence. If he then commits suicide he confesses
by that act that death is the meaning of existence; by the sacrifice of
his life to death his life gains significance. Distraught or confused,
sometimes insane or sometimes perverted, as the man committing
suicide may be, he still harbors the vanity that there is something he

can do to render his existence of decisive moral significance, something he can do to find justification. Even the man who despairs of any meaning in life this side of death nurses hope in the tribute and service that he can perform for the power of death by killing himself. He is still not utterly helpless.

To become and be absolutely helpless the man at the brink of suicide must give up all things, including the strange, distorted hope for justification that he has in death. To be helpless in the sense which is the inauguration of faith involves a man's confession that he cannot even help himself by destroying his own life, any more than he can in the fantasy existence of trying to justify himself by learning much, acquiring property, grasping power, raising a family, making money, being loyal, honest, charitable, kind or otherwise virtuous, abstaining from the popular vices, or indulging in good works.

There is a parable of this issue in the motion picture "The Seventh Seal," one of Ingmar Bergman's films. The story is about a young knight from Sweden obsessed with his own search for God. The knight, as the movie opens, has returned from the Crusades, where he had gone in quest of God but through which he had not found God. Now he comes home and beholds the Church engaged, as portrayed in the story, in violent rites of exorcism against those who were victims of the black plague. He sees a great procession through the streets in which those diseased of the plague are being flogged by the clergy in order to be freed from their affliction. He concludes that, wherever God might be located, He is not likely to be found in a church engaged in such brutalities. The remainder of the film recounts certain adventures and experiences the knight has as he perseveres in his search for God. The episodes are various and the knight's moods are too — sometimes he is depressed, sometimes defiant, sometimes desperate, sometimes demanding, sometimes confident that he is close to his destination. In the climax of each episode he always comes back to his obsession — "Where is God?" — "What must I do to find God?" — "If God is, let Him show me His face!" And each time that, in a variety of ways, he asks his question, he does indeed see a face, but each time the face that he beholds is the face of death and not the face of God.

The movie dramatizes the essential issue of asking in faith for faith. The knight is an earnest and deeply religious man. He devotes his life to the religious quest. Yet his search discovers only death because the very pursuit of God presupposes that God may only be known in response to human initiative of one sort or another. Any image of God which is, thus, dependent upon man's enterprise is not the living God and, even though literally true in its insight into the nature of God, is, in fact, an image of death. The knight, the sincere religious man, is, in reality, a profound atheist because the very search for God is a denial of God's existence and of God's integrity as God. The affirmation of the quest is that God exists only in the mind, imagination or hallucination of men. In order to behold the face of God, the knight must give up his question, abandon his search for God, forsake religion. He must become and be utterly helpless: he must acknowledge and know in his whole being, intellectually, viscerally, physically, that there is nothing at all that he can do to establish relationship with God, nothing that he can do to save himself, and that all attempts to the contrary end in the appearance of death in the place of God.

This estate of unconditional helplessness in all things is the primitive experience of faith because it is the unqualified recognition that if God lives, He is His own self, existing, acting and working freely, apart from any dependence or control or convenience or appeasement or manipulation of any man or institution, including the several religions as well as the Church, or, for that matter, anything whatever. The veracity of God's existence and of His care for the life of this world is, as it were, a burden that belongs wholly to God. The utter helplessness that causes a man to know no more than that, is a man's elementary suffering of the meaning of his own mere humanity, on one hand, and of the godliness of God, on the other. Whatever specific circumstances may be involved — remembering that there are no stereotyped, *pro forma* circumstances ever involved — the whole existence of a man, from the very moment of his conception in a womb, indeed, from his creation in the Word of God, is exposed at once to the fullness of death's power and to the presence of God affirming his whole being despite the power of death. How-

ever time be accounted in these circumstances — remembering that the
category of time is shattered in such travail — it is, so to speak, then
and there, in the helplessness from which there is absolutely no human
or other worldly recourse — when there is nowhere to turn, no place
to hide, no escape, nothing that can be done — that it is given to a
man to know that it is God alone who rescues and raises men from
the clutches of death in this life. It is, thus, that a man becomes beneficiary to the secret that the Resurrection of Christ is no myth, nor
tale of something that happened once upon a time and has no reference
or relevance to the present day and to his own life, but is, rather, the
singular event of all history, breaching and resolving the mystery of
a man's own particular identity as a person. It is in this way — in
dying to the preposterous arrogance of trying to save one's self, in
surrender of each and every futile anxiety to justify one's self, in the
risk of the loss of life altogether, in the midst of the awful militancy
of death, in utter helplessness — that life is restored to a man.

Faith is a charismatic gift. Faith is that most peculiar gift of
God acting in this world which is offered to every human being and
is the synonym of life itself. No man may receive that gift who
supposes that it is, in any sense, deserved, and who, therefore, doubts
that it is a gift in the first instance. No man welcomes such a gift
who has not become forlorn of any hope in every other promise of
salvation. No man suffers such an awesome and generous gift who
has not already endured all that death can do to him. No man is established in faith (and thus renewed in life) who has not descended
into that utter helplessness in which only God can render help.

No man is a Christian — which means, simply, to be a real
human being — who has not thus asked in faith for faith.

Coercion vs. Faith

The gift of faith is inherently associated with crisis. Faith,
indeed, concerns the only crisis that human beings confront in this
world: *death*. All specific crises — birth, loneliness, lust, illness, both
success and failure, age, accident, conflict, scandal — only foreshadow
death and all of them are consummated in death. In that sense, death
is appropriately regarded as not only the final crisis, but the immediate

crisis of existence. In the Gospel, faith is about the evident reign of the power of death in this world and the possibility of the transcendence of death in this life.

It is thought vulgar to mention death so blandly. Death is not even accorded the honor due death at funerals, much less being recognized unabashedly as the apparent ruling idol of life. Yet it is obvious that death survives all other powers, apart from God, in this world. By death, I refer, of course, to biological extinction and to death as the destination of life, but, at the same time, much more than that. Death, both biblically and empirically, denominates the moral reality in this world that is greater than any other reality to which men attach significance for their existence, leaving God aside. Death not only outlasts money, virtue, fame, sex, religion or the other idols but death is the idol of all other idols. Death is the obvious meaning of existence, if God is ignored, surviving as death does every other personal or social reality to which is attributed the meaning of existence in this world. Death is so great, so aggressive, so pervasive and so militant a power that the only fitting way to speak of death is similar to the way one speaks of God. Death is the living power and presence in this world which feigns to be God.

The gift of faith involves enduring the full assault of the power of death in one's own life in relationship to the claim of death over all of life and, in the same event, suffering the power of God overcoming death in one's own existence in relation to the rest of creation. Faith is bestowed in the death in Christ. The man of faith, in a Christian sense, is the man who has already, in the midst of this life, been exposed to all that death can do and been raised to life, emancipated from death's rule and from all the more puny idols that are the suffragans of death.

Because the gift of faith — conversion, to use one of the traditional terms — is always associated with crisis and because all crises are aggressions of the power of death, there is a terrible and constant temptation that human beings will be manipulated or coerced by professing Christians in the name of "converting" them. That peril is perhaps most blatant in the precincts of so-called mass evangelism, and this is one of the reasons that I have earlier suggested that this activity is not evangelism but, at best, revivalism. It is, for example, part of the established procedure in Billy Graham's crusades to call upon the people assembled to raise their hands if they desire to be committed or recommitted to Christ. If, thereafter, when the invitation comes to go forward to the platform to enact that wish, there are those who have shown their hands but hesitate to make the journey down the aisle, they are visited by spotters located throughout the premises who urge them to do so. The risk of exploiting troubled people, the possibilities of vitiating free choice, the probabilities of precipitating traumatic experience are so manifest in such circumstances that I, for one, consider them to be wholly sufficient to warrant the abandonment entirely of such "crusades."

The temptation to coerce "faith" is present in other ways in addition to "mass evangelism" campaigns, for instance, where a person's insecurities in personality or practical life are manipulated by appeals to prejudice, the anxiety for success, the profit motive and the like. The danger then is that "faith" is induced by fraudulent promises of personal aggrandizement through self-help in the practice of "prayer" and "positive thinking."

Coercion is common, too, where popular fears about social change, moral laxity, or the threat of Communism are exploited as reasons for joining and supporting a church. This is no different in principle than the old-time preachers who threatened damnation to any who would not conform and believe.

Christians are not called upon to assault other human beings, in these or similar ways, in the name of saving them. Besides, no Christian ever converted any other person. Authentic conversion is a work of Christ, not of Christians or of the Church, as the Bible abundantly testifies. Faith cannot be coerced. It is a matter of grace in much the same fashion as the love of one person for another is a gift. Faith is not something so cheap that it may be purchased by any effort, not something rewarded for any merit, not something gained for the seeking, however earnest, but a thing, on the contrary, that is ridiculed by pietism, thwarted by religion, and opposed guilefully by death. It is God's grace that establishes a man in faith, that is, reconciles a man within himself and with the whole of creation.

Learning vs. Faith

Faith is to be distinguished from coerced confessions and from emotional, sentimental, or visceral responses to threats or inducements. Faith is also distinct from mere intellectual assent to creeds or doctrines, from learning in an academic or catechismal sense, and from vigorous conviction. Whether or not any of these notions of faith have any partial validity in the Gospel, none of them represent faith as a charismatic gift. Faith, in the meaning described here, as the crisis of death in Christ, does not issue from either ecstatic experience or pedantic knowledge.

That does not imply that to be a Christian requires one to be nonsensical or to neglect to engage the intelligence in the exposition and practice of the Christian faith. It just means that the Gospel is *not* essentially ideational or conceptionalistic or speculative. Theology is not the same thing as ideology. Faith is categorically different from adherence to a philosophic point of view. Faith is an event in the drama of life in this world, much the same as love is, encompassing the intellect, but not restricted by the intellect. Faith as a gift implicates the whole person: the mind, by all means, but the feelings and guts of men as well.

The vigor of modern scientism and the challenges to Christian faith of secular ideology and of the various religions have, legitimately, pressed Christians to more rigorous apologetics for the Gospel and have, happily, rid the Church to some extent of the anti-intellectualism that burdened American Christendom, for one example, in the era of the Scopes trial about the teaching of Darwinian evolutionary theories. The churches and sects are not wholly freed from this handicap yet, but, insofar as they have been emancipated, they have tended to be overly zealous to demonstrate the intellectual respectability of the Christian faith by treating the content of the Gospel in a merely pedantic fashion. Thus, the Gospel is very commonly regarded among the clergy as a theoretical corpus that stands side by side with ideological, religious and philosophical systems as one of a kind, and, to the believer, presumably, is the best of the lot.

I recall, a few years ago, serving on a commission of the Episcopal Church charged with articulating the scope of the total ministry of the Church in modern society. The commission numbered about forty persons, a few laity and the rest professional theologians, ecclesiastical authorities and clergy. The group met, in the course of a year and a half, three times for sessions of more than a week. The first conference, as I recall it, floundered in churchy shoptalk that anyone outside the Church would find exasperatingly irrelevant, largely incoherent or simply dull. Toward the end of that meeting some of those present proposed that it might be an edifying discipline for the group, in its future sessions, to undertake some concentrated study of the Bible. It was suggested that constant recourse to the Word of God in the Bible is as characteristic and significant a practice in the Christian life as the regular participation in the celebration of the Eucharist, which was a daily observance of this commission. Perhaps, it was argued, Bible study would enlighten the deliberations of the commission and, in any event, would not impede them.

The proposal was rejected on the grounds, as one Bishop present put it, that "most of us have been to seminary and know what the Bible says: the problem now is to apply it to today's world." The Bishop's view was seconded (with undue enthusiasm, I thought at the time) by the Dean of one of the Episcopal seminaries as well as by the clergy bureaucrats from national headquarters who had, they explained, a program to design and administer.

I recount this episode without assessing the decision of the overwhelming majority of that commission opposing Bible study. I am not the judge, though it would be difficult for me to conclude that any harm could have come from opening the Book and trying to listen to the Word. The only point in mentioning the incident here, however, is that the notion implied in the decision not to engage in Bible study is that the Gospel, in its Biblical embodiment, is of an essentially pedantic character — a static body of knowledge which, once systematically organized, taught and learned, has use ceremonially, sentimentally, nostalgically, and as a source from which deductions can be made to guide the religious practice and ethical conduct of contemporary Christians. If that is what the Bible is, then it is generically undistinguished from religious scripture of any sort and, for that matter, is of no more dignity than any secular ideology or philosophy.

If that is what the Bible is, then it is a dead word and not the Living Word.

Such a view of the Bible authorizing, evidently, a merely academic use of the Bible, if pressed to its final logic, challenges the versatility and generosity of God's revelation of Himself in history and is a form of doubt deplored in James (cf. 1:5-8; 3:13-4:6).

Yet that very way of regarding the Bible is not only current among ecclesiastical authorities or seminary professionals, it has gained a wide acceptance in the last decade or so in programs of lay theological education in the several denominations and interdenominationally. The innumerable conferences, institutes, faith and life programs, lay academies conducted have generally been geared to the idea that to be a conscientious Christian in a secular occupation or profession requires a layman to be academically indoctrinated with theology. I have no objection to the laity — or the clergy and hierarchy — becoming theologically literate; my concern is whether in that pursuit theology becomes stagnant and the laity sterile, incapable of existential encounter with the vitality of the Biblical Word.

Indeed the perils, in the nurture of the laity, in the mere academization of theology, where that is accompanied by the continued neglect of the Bible, are as great, to my mind, as the superstitious and romanticized uses typical of the "prayer breakfasts" among some laymen's movements. The former distorts the Gospel because it is too theoretical; the latter perverts the Gospel by being too visceral; both stand in contrast to the event of faith as charismatic gift.

In part, I suspect the recent emphasis on pedantic theological training for laymen in many churches is an over-compensation for abysmal collapse, finally, of the "Sunday School." The inherited "Sunday School" institutions have been educationally archaic for generations by virtually any measure taken of them: plant and teaching aids, qualification of instructors, time allotted for classroom work, teacher-student ratio, curriculum content and design. More than that, the increasing sophistication of secular education in the elementary and secondary schools has exposed the futility of much of what has been happening in the "Sunday School." You cannot recite religious fairy tales in church to a child who is learning the new math in school. You cannot inculcate the old pietistic moralism in youth for whom modern communications has convincingly shown such pietism to be ridiculously irrelevant and, in any case, neither believed nor practiced in adult society, by their "Sunday School" teachers, their ministers, or their parents. Yet the failure of the inherited "Sunday School" institution does not justify the kind of excessive, exclusive academization of "Christian education" that is now becoming evident in adult laymen's programs and in the revamping provoked by the crisis in the "Sunday Schools."

It is not the intention here to embark on any exhaustive critique of the foibles and failures of the nurture of the churches of either youth or adults, though I would be inclined to abandon most existing "Sunday School" efforts and to dismantle most laymen's "theological education" enterprises. All that is, however, here affirmed is that the primary reliance in the nurture of the Christian people must be upon the Bible and, as has been mentioned earlier, upon a fresh, spontaneous, unencumbered access to the Word in the Bible. It happens that the Christian people in this day, in this land at least, have available to them modern translations of the Bible, in the language of their time and society, that are unprecedented for their accuracy, lucidity and scholarly competence in translation. Christians today have perhaps the most trustworthy access to the Biblical Word since the very days of the oral tradition from which the Bible took form and was authorized. The first recourse, therefore, must be to the Bible — in all so-called Christian education, as well as in preaching and the liturgical life.

Doublemindedness

The peril in the mere academization of theology is that theology is treated as an abstract, ideational, theoretical schema disassociated from the confession of the faith. The risk is not so much heresy as it is agnosticism. Theologizing which is pedantic may be quite literally true but still unrelated to the personal disposition of the "theologian." Thus I would insist that all authentic theology is not only a definition and elucidation of the Gospel but is also indispensably a confession of the Gospel for the one who speaks theologically and a proclamation of the Gospel to those who hear.

It is this issue which James refers to in the passage about how the "doubleminded man" will receive no gift of faith from the Lord.

It is this same matter that, I observe, makes Karl Barth such a threatening and unnerving figure among the professional theologians.

Karl Barth's pre-eminence among theologians of the present century is such as to make mention of his credentials vulgar. Yet Barth himself repeatedly affirms that he is no Barthian, that there is no such thing — properly speaking — as a Barthian, that he has constructed no theological system, that he has no peculiar interpretation or school of thought of his own. Since he has constructed no theology in his own name, he has no position as such to either assert or defend, and if he is freed from bondage to the hobgoblin of consistency. For him to speak theologically is indistinguishable from confessing the Gospel.

This is made possible, even for one who is a learned professor of theology, by the very integrity of the Word of God as such, which has identity, content and vitality that can be, by the grace of the Word of God, discerned, enjoyed, proclaimed, expounded, defended by men.

Thus, Barth maintains that what he says and writes theologically suffers the discipline of the Word of God. It is, as he once put it, as if the Word of God were constantly "looking over the shoulder" of the theologian — rather than the other way around, rather than if the theologian were, in his theology, disciplining the Word of God !

There is a sense in which Karl Barth is not only not a Barthian, but he is not a theologian either, save in the sense in which any Christian is a "theologian" — that is, in which he beholds all things as part and parcel of the living drama of God's Word in this world and bespeaks his own witness in his own way to the saga of the Word of God in history. For Barth, the work of theology is a confessional act, not a speculative exercise. Theology — unlike the traditional academic subjects — is not essentially a particular accomplishment of human science, but the marvel of the Word of God addressing men in ordinary history. Hence Barth entitles his most momentous work *Church Dogmatics,* which has the meaning of confession of the Church, rather than, for instance, *Systematic Theology,* which has the connotation of some concoction of his own.

All of this, in Barth's vocation in the present time, has made him a controversial and somewhat unwelcome figure among both academic theologians and ecclesiastical professionals in the churches, in America and elsewhere in the world. After all, if he would only grant that his work represented only his own reflection and insight, then it could be classified among other interesting ideas, but others would be relieved of contending with the singular thrust of Barth's witness: *there is a Word of God militant and available to human beings here and now, and all of life in this world possesses significance in that Word* (cf. James 1:18-21).

This obstinancy of Karl Barth, in his own witness, in insisting upon the independence of the Word of God in this world is dramatized, by contrast, in my experience by a relationship that I have with a gentleman who occupies an endowed professorship in theology in a distinguished American seminary. He is a thoroughly competent scholar, as such things are measured, erudite in many matters, attentive to the views of others, prolific in his own words, possessed of a social conscience that has some vigor, a lucid instructor, an active citizen, a fascinating conversationalist. He and I have been well acquainted for a dozen years and there exists between us a continuing but repetitious discourse about theology — a kind of floating debate aptly compared to a game. A typical conversation between us will run like this: I will remark about something — often an attempt to theologize about the contemporary social crisis in America. Almost invariably he will respond by saying, in effect, "Well, that's the sort of thing so-and-so said in such-and-such a century." So-and-so commonly turns out to be an obscure saint of whom I have barely, if ever, heard and, not being an historian, I can seldom readily identify the cultural or churchly milieu of the period mentioned.

In this fashion our discourse is aborted and fails to become dialogue. It may be, for all I know, that someone else, somewhere else did utter something similar to my own view, but the identification and classification of my thinking according to its resemblance to that of others is unresponsive. I want my friend to respond, to dispute, to contend, to commit himself, to confess himself, but, as it seems to me, all he will ever do is catalogue my position. He is, by the conventional credentials, an illustrious professional theologian, but I fear that he is, in reality, a librarian: a classifier of material. He catalogues ideas, trends, schools of thought generically and chronologically, he can compare and contrast one with another, but he forebears to take any position himself. For him — in sharp contrast to Barth — the work of theology is not in itself a confessional event for the theologian, but a matter of academic technique. Perhaps it is this form of doubt, this doublemindedness, this paralysis of commitment — prevalent, I dare say, among pedantic theologians — which accounts for the admonition, elsewhere in James, that those who become teachers shall be judged with greater strictness (James 3:1).

The "death of God" movement is associated with this same concern over doublemindedness, but it has become so much more a journalistic episode than an effort to clarify and discipline academic theology that it seems destined to defeat its own best intention. The very notoriety of the so-called death of God theology, unfortunately, obscures most significant issues in contemporary churchly life and, paradoxically, camouflages the essential difference between the Gospel of Christ and religion of any sort, discussed at length earlier in this book.

What are the death of God "theologians" saying?

If they are saying that the inherited churchly institutions of a divided and sectarian Christendom are preposterously irrelevant and virtually incapacitated in ministering to the world, they have massive and probably conclusive evidence to support the allegation. The denominational churches *are* dying. Kierkegaard foresaw that a century ago.

If these voices are asserting that acculturated conceptions of God are inappropriate and impotent, they are categorically correct. They are also very tardy with the news, since St. Paul made that the theme of a sermon to the Athenians nineteen centuries ago.

If these self-styled radicals are arguing that institutional religion is no longer worthy of the allegiance of men, they are quite right, though that is hardly a revelation since the ministry of Christ Himself in this world made mere religion trivial and obsolete.

If they are, on the other hand, propounding, as *Time* magazine reports that they are, some "new" idea of God fitted to twentieth-century secular life, then they are pathetically confused. They are imitating the very thing against which they complain with such vehemence. This century's ideas of God, or ideas of no God or non-ideas of God have no more significance or tenure than those of the Puritan era or the Victorian age or the Rennaisance or the pre-Reformation era, or of any other time.

What the "death of God" movement authentically could expose is the radical, original, Biblical distinction between religion and the Gospel. It could show the futility of the human search for God. It could demonstrate how even the most profound religious quest is unnecessary. It could affirm that Christians propound no idea of God at all but instead behold the vitality of the Word of God in history. It could emphasize that the uniqueness of the Gospel, as distinguished from religion, is in the celebration of God's initiative rather than concentration upon man's religious quest. Unhappily all of this has been submerged in self-serving forensics over a slogan that whatever journalistic interest it bears, is incoherent, unbiblical and irrelevant for Christian witness in the world.

Yet, by the virtue of Christ, the truths remain: all inherited churchly institutions are decadent, all religions are obsolete, and all ideas of God are dead. And by the veracity of Christ's historic witness only a doubleminded man, unstable in his ways, worships a church or religion or any idea of God in the place of the living God.

The Independence of the Word of God

It is one thing to complain about the superficiality of the "death of God" debate, chastise academic theologians for only being religious philosophers, or recognize Karl Barth as a preacher, discern that "Sunday School" is a ridiculous anachronism, protest the rejection of reliance upon the Bible by eminent ecclesiastics, or fear that many are coerced in the name of faith. It is another matter to affirm the Word of God present in Jesus Christ, accept that same presence "implanted" in all of life throughout all history, agree that the Word of God disciplines theology — rather than the other way around — distinguish the Word of the Gospel from religions of all varieties, and declare that faith is a charismatic gift freeing men here and now from the power of death (cf. James 1:21).

One may readily concur in all of the former, without being persuaded at all about any of the latter.

If faith cannot be achieved in any sense, how shall faith be known — and, indeed, how shall the faithful know who they are? How, to put it differently, does anyone apprehend the Word of God as such? How can it be understood that the Word of God is wholly other than the words of men, yet incessantly addressed to men in their common life? If religion is obviated, if the churches are too much surrendered to idolatry, if *all* ideas of God are dead, how is the integrity and objectivity of the Word of God discerned by ordinary folk in the practical circumstances of existence?

In deference to the Biblical witness, such questions are most appropriately dealt with in parable, that is, by reciting an actual incident in which the liveliness of the Word of God is disclosed.

Sometime ago the rector of a certain parish in New York City invited me to undertake instruction of the high school age "Sunday School" class of the congregation. He belabored the troubles that had accompanied the attempt to have any "class" for these kids at all. The situation was that, while the parish was relatively affluent and extremely status conscious, it was located in a neighborhood in Manhattan that was changing rapidly. The older families of the parish lingered on out of sentiment or regard for the parish premises as their own monument, but their offspring were away at private schools and had no interest in either returning to the parish or raising their own families in this region. Meanwhile, others had entered the neighborhood and associated themselves with the parish, especially some of the high school students thereabouts. They were, apparently, attracted to the parish by the fact that it had a fully equipped gymnasium and an adequately appointed swimming pool. Together these constituted the only available recreational facilities of the sort in the area. The rector, thus, explained to me that the parish had the "problem" of somehow dealing with these neighborhood urchins — whose parents, if any, had nothing to do, as he put it, with the congregation — while the secondary school children of the parish were away at one or another boarding school, unable to utilize the facilities originally provided for them. An accommodation of sorts had, he informed me, been already reached. The teenagers from the immediate environs were allowed access to the gym and pool, for dances and sports during weekdays, if they also, on Sundays, attended with regularity "Sunday School." Would I, he entreated me, take on that "Sunday School class"? Other "teachers" had found the local kids very difficult to discipline or instruct, but, he said, he knew that from my work as a lawyer in East Harlem, I had some experience with these folk, both adults and adolescents, and perhaps, he thought, I could manage the "class" in question.

So I became a "Sunday School" teacher.

I was soon supplied with the curriculum material that the rector proposed to have used in this group. It was one of the so-called new curriculums of Christian education that have been developed in recent years in most of the major denominations. I reviewed this stuff very carefully. I found it to be objectionable, not only because it presupposed that the "student" would be a white Anglo-Saxon of the middle classes, but also because it was in several parts plainly heretical, if, at least, one regards the Bible as definitive of the Word of God lively in this world. Moreover, I soon learned that no more than forty-five minutes per Sunday, for no more than two dozen Sundays of the year, were to be devoted to this enterprise.

I regretted my commitment to the rector, because on the face of it the whole effort seemed so absurd. There was not enough time allowed to succeed in teaching much of anything about much of anything, and it was so denigrating — that is, shall teenagers, already educationally deprived, commonly bereft of parents, unfamiliar with the Church or anyway misled about the Church, be now subjected to careless and erroneous indoctrinations on Sundays in exchange for occasional access to a gymnasium and swimming pool the rest of the week? Regardless of anything else, why should this sort of condition of attendance at the parish's "Sunday School" apply to use of the recreational facilities? And, if it could be rationalized, why not at least try to tell the children the truth of the Gospel instead of some idiot tale?

I asked the rector such questions. His response was that "these kids" needed to learn their place, to experience some quiet and some discipline, and that, after all, the parish was not there, where it was, in a changing neighborhood, just to be used by those who contributed nothing to its continuance.

I asked myself the same questions. I considered that, if I were to do this at all, I could not submit to the rector's apparent rejection of the youth involved, nor use the curriculum provided, nor make attendance in "class" a condition of weekday recreation at the parish facilities, nor confine my relationship with the "students" to Sunday morning for forty-five minutes. All of that I considered. All of that, I concluded, would have to change.

The rector admonished me that the "students" were sometimes rebellious, and he emphasized the need to be stern and demanding of them. They must be regular and timely in attendance, their presence must be duly recorded, they must do homework, they must be quiet enough so as not to disrupt the practice of the salaried choir in an adjacent room, they must not disturb the other Sunday functions of the parish, they must be made to dress "respectably," they must behave — which meant, as I heard the rector on the occasion, that they must be as inconspicuous as if they virtually did not exist. That was what was really wanted. If that condition were met, then these same kids could have a dance or play basketball or take a swim at the parish facilities.

In fairness, it should be mentioned that the minister had had problems with the youth in question which, no doubt, made him nervous and inclined toward making rules. There had been, for example, the time, one Sunday, when these young people had come, as a crowd, to the church earlier than usual and had loitered in the chapel separate from the main sanctuary, had smoked cigarettes there and — presumably for want of an ashtray — had snuffed out their butts in the baptismal font in that chapel, only to have their misdeed promptly discovered by the sexton and, soon after that, by the rector. To the clergyman, it seemed at once to be some great sacrilege (the sexton, I recall, was rather amused by the audacity). Dire utterances were delivered to the offenders and they were denied the advantage of "Sunday School" and the access to the gym for quite awhile after the incident. As far as I could figure out, nobody bothered to inquire whether this was a prank or protest, assuming that the two can be significantly distinguished.

Anyway, I undertook the "class."

Since I could not conscientiously use the "new curriculum" materials that had been furnished, I had first to determine what could be responsibly employed with those whom I was somehow to address as a teacher. I decided to rely upon the Bible.

On the day of the first session of the "class" the meeting lasted only long enough for each to announce to the rest his name and for me to say that I had, on my own authority, decided to discard the curricular materials that had been provided by the parish, and that, since we were all under some sanction or other to continue to meet, I proposed that we spend the time together reading the Bible, and hopefully, we might even become free enough to listen to the Word of the Bible. Since, however, the class was not to use the curriculum procured and paid for by the parish, since that was now being repudiated and thrown away because it was undeserving of attention, it was further directed, on that first Sunday, that each member of the "class" obtain a copy of the Revised Standard Version of the New Testament. Information as to the availability of paperback editions of the New Testament in this translation was supplied.

Now these were "students" who had seldom ever purchased or read any book, and to tell them to go out and buy a copy of the New Testament for use in this "class" was, I realized, asking a lot, so it did not surprise me that on the second Sunday, and on the third and, again, on the fourth, none of them had complied with my directions. Yet, during that time all of them — there were thirteen in all — did dispose of the authorized "Sunday School" books and all of them submitted, if reluctantly, to my conduct of the "class" during this, as it were, interim period. All that happened, and all that was allowed, in the brief sessions of the "class" following that first Sunday, was that I read, aloud, the entire Letter to the Romans. Interruptions were

ruled out of order; questions were forbidden; the meetings were conducted in a most arbitrary manner in which the only thing permitted
was the reading of the Letter, the utterance of the Word as such according to the testimony of Romans. Kids in the "class" who com-
plained about this procedure or who lapsed into unfortunate habits
of earlier "Sunday School" experiences were simply and repeatedly
confronted with the insistence that this "class" was going to engage
in Bible study, that to do so it had repudiated the conventional and
prescribed curriculum and conduct of the "class," and that until every
student in the group was equipped with a copy of the New Testament
and could thus participate directly in reading Romans, the time, each
Sunday, would be wholly utilized in the Letter being read to them
aloud.

Apparently the message penetrated, after several weeks, because
the young people did acquire copies of the New Testament and appeared in "class" with them and began ostensibly to follow along as
the Letter was read. Meanwhile, there were other problems in the
course of action I had elected. It was, for example, the custom of
this "Sunday School" to take attendance by having the curate of the
parish visit each "class" in session each week. This was, in my view,
an intolerable invasion of the already too little time allowed. It was
a stupid and officious procedure with which, before long, I declined
to cooperate. I refused to permit this weekly census to be taken in
my "class" under the sanction — the only one available to me — that
the "class" would be entirely disbanded if the harassment continued.
To that ultimatum the clergy of the parish reluctantly acceded.

No sooner had that little crisis been endured when there was
rebellion in the "class." One morning the boy whom a social psy-
chologist would characterize as the "natural leader" of the "class"
appeared on the scene lugging under his arm a case of beer — a left-
over, he explained, from an all-night party from which he was returning. The other "students" were delighted, it seemed to me, with his
bravado in bringing beer into the premises of the church, and thus
supposedly defiling the premises. Confronted by the boy, I suggested
that he fetch a church key — a can opener — so that we could all
enjoy the refreshment he had brought with him. For that "Sunday

School" lesson, we all just sat around and sipped beer, to, I do believe, the staggering frustration of the boy whose challenge had solicited rejection.

After the beer incident, the "class" went somewhat easier. Some of the girls in it volunteered to share the work of reading, but the essential event each week remained the same — all of us simply heard a reading of the entire Letter to the Romans. It was only after the group had suffered this exercise a dozen or more times, week after week, that the tactic was changed and I proposed that the Letter be then read sentence by sentence, in its given sequence, and that after reading each sentence aloud, we all pause and ask one question: *What does this say?* Not, what do I think? Not, do I agree? Not, is this relevant to my life and circumstances? But, straightforwardly, first of all, *What is this word?*

So we persevered. It was a laborious enterprise. But we did continue, meeting each Sunday, and, as it were, reading and listening to each sentence of Romans, in turn, and asking, What is being said?

Silence — utter, unequivocal, radical, dumbfounded silence — greeted this practice for weeks. But I insisted upon it and the members of the "class" acquiesced in it, as much out of bemusement at this unorthodox "Sunday School" as anything, I suppose.

It was around Christmastime that the change came. The same boy who had brought the case of beer to "class" turned up one afternoon at my tenement in East Harlem. He was, it seemed to me, embarrassed to appear to have deliberately come to visit me and belabored a number of excuses for dropping in. Finally, after his protracted and circumlocuacious introit, he mentioned that he had obtained a copy of the New Testament (he had stolen it, he boasted, from the premises of some other church) and confessed that he had been listening in "class," though he had not spoken out there, during all the weeks in which Romans had been repeatedly read aloud. He thought, he said, that I must have plenty of other things to do and would not bother to take time for this "class" or persist in reading the Letter in "class" unless I was convinced there was something important in the Letter. His curiosity was engaged and he had procured a New Testament, he admitted, in order to read the Letter on his own

in his privacy. He had now some reflections about his own comprehension of Romans that he wanted to discuss because he had wondered
if my own understanding of the Letter corresponded with his.

For the remainder of that afternoon he and I tried to talk with
one another about our respective experiences of hearing the Word of
God in and through the Letter to the Romans.

This tough, brash, aggressive kid from the streets turned out, in
that encounter, to be a most sophisticated exegete, although I am
pretty sure that if I ever called him such to his face his impulse would
be to hit me for cussing him. Somehow it had lingered in his conscience that the original, indispensible and characteristic question to
ask, in reading the Bible, is the very question that seems so seldom to
be asked in church or seminary or layman's conferences, namely, *What
does this say?* Somehow, thus, he had come, reluctantly, against
his will, with his customary hostility and suspicion, to confront the
Word of God in the Bible in a way very similar to that in which he
would face another person. In the relentless and brutal actualities of
his daily existence in the neighborhood, he had long since learned
that he must challenge everyone to speak for themselves — his peers,
the cops, school teachers and social workers, the minister, his parents
and brothers and sisters. He insisted, in meeting other human beings,
upon a word that would identify the other in relation to him; he
sought from others a word that embodied a commitment one way or
another about his existence and presence within the sound and upon
the scene of the word being uttered. Somehow, now, he had been
coming to terms with the Biblical Word in a fashion quite like the
way he was accustomed to receiving people, and to knowing whether
they were friends or enemies or merely indifferent toward him. Somehow, now, he was enabled by the authority of his own everyday effort
of survival as a person to open the Letter to the Romans and both
await and expect the Word to be spoken and also stop and listen to
that Word in its own context and for its own merit, without preconceptions or neatness or anything to prove. Somehow the very serious-
ness of his own involvement in his own world as he knew it was the
very substance of his innocence toward the Word of God in the Bible

and the credential that freed him to listen to the Biblical Word and marvel.

During the afternoon's conversation, I realized the boy was telling me what he had heard of the Word of God, not what his opinion or desire about the Word might be. In that sense, he was speaking as a true witness, in the strict meaning of the term, of what he had beheld at first hand, without evaluation, speculation, tampering or embellishment.

I do not know whether in his private encounter with Romans he had suffered conversion or whether that was the news he had come to tell me. That is only something for him to mention. But I am confident that he had endured the disclosure and discovery of the independence of the Word of God, mediated through his adventure with the Letter, though I am fully persuaded that there are few, if any, conversions to the Gospel of Christ that are not associated with just such exposure of a person to the living Word.

And, in any case, I am sure that his confrontation with the Word in Romans had been such that he now knew that "God" is not some fairy tale contrived by adults to more conveniently suppress youth, some intimidating ruse to keep adolescents docile — which was the essential idea propagated theretofore in that "Sunday School"; or, on the other hand, that "God" designates some fantasy to substitute for sensible explanation of the profound mystery of death and life in this world, some illusion to shield folk from the harsh and wonderful realities of ordinary existence. Whatever the ultimate truth of his personal encounter with the Word in the Bible, he had been emancipated enough, I know, to see something of how different the Word of God is in both content and conduct from preposterous and pretentious religious indoctrinations supplied by churches like the parish with which both he and I were then affiliated.

Among the gifts of that afternoon with this most remarkable exegete was the illuminating candor of our own relationship. Now, for the first time, we met, under the aegis of the Word, in a new way. Now we were set free from the roles consigned to each of us or adopted by either of us in the prior contacts in "class." We were no longer restricted by differences of education or learning or race or age or class or whatnot. Now, by the virtue and initiative of the Word of God, bespoken and attended to in our respective experiences in the Letter to the Romans, each of us became at liberty not only to praise the integrity of the Word of God but to be accused and convicted in our own identities as individuals. It was, that afternoon, not just that the Word of God was, as it were, recognized as a name, but that each of us also were named ourselves in the very same happening. Now the Word of God, in the testimony of Romans, became evident as the event in which each of us were more certainly and fully our selves (cf. James 1:18; 1:21).

Part of the wonder of the occasion was and is that when and wherever the Word of God is heard and honored, human life acquires context, people are radically distinguished and identified, community is wrought, and reconciliation happens.

Returning, subsequently, to "Sunday School" was easy and eager for this boy and myself; I suspect it was a bit startling for the class. He was the "ring leader" after all, his authority long established and uncontested, the rebel. Now he became, in fact, the teacher, causing the other members of the group to imitate his own enthusiasm for — of all things — Bible study. And so, through the winter and spring, the "class" labored on in its attempt to listen to the Word in Romans.

We did not get very far into the Letter. When the last session came, we were still in the midst of the fourth chapter, still reading the Letter sentence by sentence, sometimes, literally, word by word, still persevering in asking, *What is being said?* Yet there was extra-ordinary excitement in the enterprise and something of the integrity and substance of the Word was communicated to each of us.

The Word that was being heard was the Word of unequivocal grace, of gratuitous acceptance, of judgment coincident with forgive-ness (cf. James 2:12-13). This was a Word that these kids had seldom, if ever, suffered before in their lives and the virtual opposite of that which they had come to associate with church. No longer was "Sunday School" some penalty exacted for access to the gymnasium and, indeed, no longer was the dialogue that gradually matured in Bible study confined to the minutes allotted on the parish calendar for "class." Often, during the weekdays or on Saturdays, we would meet in my household, and I found that I was welcomed in their homes and haunts. Some began to attend the early morning celebration of the Holy Communion in the parish and to discern that the ancient liturgy enacted there was in itself a dramatization of the Word in the Bible. Some were confirmed as communicants. One, while still coming to "class," began again to go to Mass in the Roman Catholic parish of his childhood. Usually the "class" would gather in a nearby coffee shop, an hour or so before the session at the church, and invariably most everyone lingered on after the time in which "Sunday School" was supposed to be dismissed. And, as this modest new community was being constituted, its interest and conversations embraced the practical lives of its members. So we were free to speak of the mystery of the presence of the Word of God in common life, enlightened by our adventure of beholding the same Word in the Bible.

If I had harbored any doubts about the affection for the Word that had grown up among these young people, they were dispelled the following fall. The rector had asked me once again to take the "class" of this age group. I had agreed, and I had decided to follow essentially the same procedure. This time, however, I chose Colossians, instead of Romans, in the thought that it might be possible to get through the whole of the shorter letter.

On the first day of "Sunday School" the six new "students" were there, but also seven of the thirteen who had been in the Romans "class." They had, of course, "graduated" from "Sunday School" the previous spring, but they announced that they wished to continue in Bible study. I had very little to do that second year. The "alumni" assumed leadership of the study of Colossians and conducted the "class" in much the same way that had eventually been established the previous year.

I recite this experience with these adolescents in Bible study not so much to be critical of the manner in which they had been regarded and treated in this particular parish by other adults, including the minister — though I think they had been dealt with shamefully and insensitively. Nor am I specifically commending a "teaching method" — in the nurture of human beings in the Gospel I think such to be gimmicky, manipulative, and radically inappropriate. Rather I am suggesting that the inherited "Sunday School" conception represents an improvident use of time, commonly propagates distortion and even heresy, stifles the Biblical Word, and obstructs the hearing of that Word. The enterprise is decadent and had better be abandoned unless and until church people, especially clergy and teachers, are free enough from petty moralism, religiosity, intolerance of youth, and churchly indoctrination to place themselves at the disposition of the Word of God in the Bible and naïve enough to listen to the Word speak. This is only a plea for honoring in church the independence of the Word of God.

I suspect that may be more difficult for adults than adolescents; harder, perchance, for clergy than laity; easier for the slum kids who were in that "class" than for anybody supposedly more sophisticated than they. Yet to confront the Word of God in such a way — in naïveté, without presuppositions or conditions, without compulsion to prove doctrine, without necessity to vindicate any opinions or conduct — is the most somber discipline of the Christian witness in this world.

Even for the Pope it is so. The issue of papal infallibility, for all the historic commotion about it, is one about which there is little difficulty if the point is made theologically rather than by lapsing into arguments for ecclesiastical monarchism. Theologically the issue is quite straightforward: the Word of God is an event in this world that has an objectivity and substance, which is addressed and communicated through the Bible *and* in the world *and* can be discerned and bespoken by human beings. The Pope, when he speaks of the Gospel, speaks under the extraordinary discipline of the independence of the Word of God, and, thus, may be said to speak infallibly. To that let it only be added and remembered that every single Christian suffers the same discipline in his own witness to the living Word.

Doubt in Faith

James entreats men to ask in faith, with no doubting, for the wisdom that is knowledge of God, knowledge of self and knowledge of all things.

There are varieties of doubt toward the Gospel, but that to which all forms of doubt are addressed is the veracity of the event of the Word of God in history. There is no separation here between the content of the Word and the occurrence of the event. The substance of the Word is indistinguishable from the action of the Word. The Word is incarnate, to use a traditional description. In any variation, doubt of the Gospel poses the question "Is this true?" in the form "Has this happened?" or "Is this taking place?"

In this sense, any doubt of the Gospel differs from doubts respecting religion or philosophy or ideology. To be in doubt about any of the latter means to be unpersuaded as to their truth, insight, intelligibility, relevance or cogency, to be in opposition to them, or sometimes simply to be ignorant or indifferent toward them.

In other words, doubts as to religion, philosophy or ideology are always related to the optional character of that which is doubted. In contrast, as James emphasizes, there is a sense in which the event of the Word of God in the world is not contingent upon apprehension, understanding, persuasion or belief, a sense in which this event is not optional, and thus, paradoxically, a sense in which any doubts about the Gospel occur *within* the context of that which is doubted.

So, in James, the brethren are urged to "receive with meekness the implanted word" (James 1:21) — to embrace that which is already embodied in their own existence, to recognize something intrinsic to their very being, to accept the event of the Word of God in history because it encompasses the fact of their own lives, to celebrate their own creation in the Word of God. So, also, James speaks of hearing the Word as observing one's real self in a mirror and denounces those who are nevertheless doubters, forgetting who they are, because they are not doers of the Word (James 1:23, 24).

There are echoes of the same understanding of the event of the Word in the world elsewhere in the Bible, notably in the Letter to the Romans:

> Ever since the creation of the world his invisible nature, namely, his eternal power and deity, has been clearly perceived in the things that have been made. So they are without excuse; for although they knew God they did not honor him as God or give

thanks to him, but they became futile in their thinking and their
senseless minds were darkened. Claiming to be wise, they became fools, and exchanged the glory of the immortal God for
images resembling mortal man or birds or animals or reptiles
(Romans 1:20-23).*

James, recalling the confrontation between Christ and Satan in
the wilderness (Matthew 4:1-11; Mark 1:12-13; Luke 4:1-13),
presses on to say, "Even the demons believe — and shudder" (James
2:19). And those who are brought forth "by the word of truth" James
names "the first fruits" of God's creatures (James 1:18).

Some may entertain doubts about the way doubt about the Gospel
is here set forth, or, at least, object that it overlooks the legions of
atheists, agnostics, and skeptics that surround the churches nowadays,
not to mention any earlier times. The answer to that is that these
forms of doubt are popularized whenever the churches are themselves
lost in those other doubts called heresy, apostasy, and idolatry.

Atheism is, at best, a radical rejection of the Word of God, and
hence a profound repudiation of human life in this world, but it is
nurtured wherever the churches proclaim heresy in word or deed,
wherever, for instance, the churches become so religious (remembering that religion is a secularization of the Gospel) that the initiative
of the Word of God in history, and, in the end, the very existence of
the Word of God in this world is denied. Heretics, in fact, are the
most convincing merchants of atheism.

Similarly, agnosticism appears to be a tenable human posture —
as opposed to faith — where apostasy is most rampant among professed Christians. That is particularly the case where the organic
divisions of the Church into sects and denominations and churches
seems empirically to belie the ecumenical vocation of the whole Christian people to become and be the pioneer of the reconciliation of the
whole of creation.

Meanwhile, skeptics of all sorts seem justified in finding the
Gospel incredible when they can plainly see that what so many churchgoers worship is some churchly institution and tradition and that an

*Cf. Ps. 19:1-4; Eph. 4:17, 18; Acts 17:29.

idol such as this is as puny and as unlike God as those of property or
status or those fashioned after reptiles or images of man.

Let the skeptics, agnostics, and atheists alone, do not persecute
or pester them, I say to fellow church people, until a day when the
conduct of those within the precincts of the churches more resembles
a society of mankind constituted in the historicity of the Word of God.
Let skeptics be popular, until idolatry is exorcised from the churches;
let agnostics abound so long as apostasy flourishes; let atheism prosper
as long as heresy is so extravagantly praised and handsomely rewarded
within the churches. Let, to put it another way, God's judgment be
notarized in the world because it is so manifest against the churches.
Let the mission of professing Christians at least not be that of only
beseeching their fellow human beings to exchange one sort of doubt
for another.

That is, I fear, about all that mission often amounts to, at least
in the familiar churches of American Christendom, as, I suspect, most
ecclesiastics and common churchgoers actually realize. If, as it evidently does, the Letter of James, in part, addresses hypocrites in the
early Church, it has a comparable audience to which to speak now, in
what, by God's mercy, may be the last days of the Church.

Perhaps the forms of doubt so prevalent in the contemporary
churches explain the kind of doubt that represents in the world a
latent faith. I have in mind, for an example, a person like Albert
Camus. How can such an extraordinary human being possibly be
regarded by a professing Christian and a church member aware of the
doubts about the event of the Word of God within the churches?

Evidenced by his writings, Camus was consumed in probing the
significance of the power of death for the meaning of life. So overwhelming is the reality of death, so dominant in daily matters, so
apparently ascendant in an ultimate sense, that, somehow, the secret
of death conceals the secret of life. So Camus pursued the matter
until his own death. Though baptized, he was not a confessing Christian, and, as far as I am aware, never became one up to the moment
of his death.

Yet surely this man must elicit much deference from Christians,
for he was acknowledging, in his life and work, that the central issue

of human existence concerns the power of death. He was, as far as is publicly known, unable to affirm, at least in traditional doctrinal terms or by means of church affiliation, the Word that in this same history the Resurrection transcends and defeats the militancy of death. Yet, at least, unlike many churchgoers, he had focused upon the essential issue, both empirically and ultimately. It has to do with the juxtapositions of life and death — not, as so many of the churchy fondly suppose, with a conflict between good and evil. It has to do with real sickness and actual healing, with the fact of alienation and the happening of reconciliation, with estrangement that is displaced by love — even and especially for one's own self, with the here and now — without anxiety about any conceivable hereafter, with living a gift not serving a penalty. At the least Camus perceived the central and profound mystery embodied in the event in this world of the Word of God. He apprehended the terrible and urgent issue to which Christian faith is the answer. Still, by his own witness, he was no Christian.

What then may be said of him? That Camus was an exceptionally mature human being — more so than could be honestly declared of many self-styled Christians, that he had outreached the realms of simplistic moralism, that he had outgrown inherited religiosity, that he rejected churchly idolatries, that he found the "elementary disputes of doctrine" boring and infantile, that he was deterred from the churches because they seemed so consummately fascinated with what is unimportant in a world in which the only truly important thing is the capability of life triumphant in the face of the imminence of death. And if a man like Camus is to be counted among those who doubt, let it be heard that his kind of doubt was a peculiar, latent, but wondrous sort of faith, and that if, in his lifetime, it did not mature to faith in the event of the Word of God in history, if it did not flower into the fullness of the stature of Christ, as St. Paul put it, then the blame is not only his; the failure also belongs, at their awful peril, to the prides and foibles of those who call themselves Christians.

Happily, on the face of the Biblical precedents, particularly that of the old Israel and, even more notoriously, that of Jesus' own disciples in the time of His earthly ministry, profession of the faith in this world, incorporated into an intentional ecclesiastical community, does not control God's love, favoritely distinguish the believer, exclude insight in an unbeliever, much less prove anybody's salvation from death.

The first chapter has already cited the Jews and how their election as a society in embassy to all mankind is not negated by doubt — whether in their hardness toward the prophetic witness or in the rejection of Christ or by renunciation of the ecumenical apostolate.

The original disciples of Jesus Christ, if anything, furnish an even more poignant instance of doubt. It is one of the extreme aberrations of the contemporary churches that the disciples are held up as exemplary Christians, when, according to the Gospels, none of them were Christians during the era of Jesus' ministry. All of them were doubters despite the repeated manifestations of the very event of the Word of God in Jesus Christ. More than that, they were — so to speak — secular doubters. They were not heretics, apostates, or churchly idolators; rather, among them were atheists, agnostics, and skeptics. They heard His parables without discernment; they beheld His authority over the power of death in temptation, in healing, in signs and miracles, in popular triumph and in agony, but they only yearned for a political messiah. They were weak, forgetful, fearful men. Some of them were ambitious, all were unreliable, one was a traitor, the rest were cowards, none of them were believers. And unbelievers — doubters — they remained through the years of His itinerancy, during the entry into the city, at the Last Supper, at Gethsemane, while He stood before Caiaphas, when Pilate condemned Him, at the foot of the Cross, even in the Resurrection, when He appeared to them in Galilee, until Pentecost.

Yet, as with the old Israel, their doubts did not estop the fidelity of God, and to them was faith given and upon them was the mission to all the world bestowed.

Chapter Three: *Temptation*

Chapter Three: TEMPTATION

*Blessed is the man who endures trial, for when he has
stood the test he will receive the crown of life which
God has promised to those who love him. Let no one
say when he is tempted, "I am tempted by God"; for
God cannot be tempted with evil and he himself
tempts no one; but each person is tempted when he is
lured and enticed by his own desire. Then desire when
it has conceived gives birth to sin; and sin when it is
full-grown brings forth death.*

James 1:12-15

Temptation has a visceral sound.

To speak the word summons images of lust and gluttony, pride
and dissipation, self-aggrandizement and vulnerability, that which is
at once seductive but forbidden. In ordinary life surrender to temptation connotes moral turpitude or, at least, malfeasance, while the
resistance to temptation seems to prove virtue or, anyway, a resolute
willpower.

Temptation has such meanings and inferences in the ethics of
the world, and is commonly rendered in a similar way in the churches.

Theologically, however, temptation is not so readily defined or
so simply understood.

81

In the Gospel temptation refers to the original and ingenious assaults of the power of death against human life, and, in James, particularly, to the aggressions of death against those professing fidelity to the event of the Word of God in history — all those, practically speaking, who call themselves Christians.

Temptation and Indulgence

In the context of James, there is a distinction between temptation in its theological significance and temptation in its mundane and moralistic meaning. The former may be, in some circumstances, co-incident with moral temptation, but the two are never mere equivalents. Faith does not embrace pietism as a synonym, though a pietistic practice may be, in a given instance, an act of faith. Temptation in its theological sense may take the guise of ordinary moral temptation but every conventional temptation does not necessarily conceal theological temptation.

It is this ambiguity of temptation understood in two different ways that helps to clarify some passages in James that seem to issue pietistic counsel while at the same time the Letter so emphatically extols the integrity of God's grace (James 1:21, cf. 2:8-13). The Bible is not free of nuance.

Insensitivity to such nuance has often caused scandal to the Gospel in what is preached, taught, and practiced in the churches. I have in mind pietism, which still flourishes in so many quarters in American Christendom: the "Bible belt" Baptist who regards dancing as consorting with the devil, the Methodist who condemns smoking categorically as sin (despite the fact that the Methodist Church and its related institutions are proportionately more heavily endowed by the philanthropy of tobacco growers and tobacco industrialists than any other ecclesiastical body in the country), some Presbyterians who regard abstinence in the use of liquor as a virtue, and a host of others from most any of the sects and denominations who think that something that human beings find pleasurable is lust and must be shunned lest the faithful be contaminated.

Pietism of this sort has legions of counterparts, though often it is not as readily recognized as when associated with sex, alcohol, tobacco or the latest dance. Recently, for instance, I came across some study material prepared for adult use in congregations of one of the big, wealthy, predominantly white, Protestant denominations located chiefly in northern states. It purported to be instruction in the meaning of the Ten Commandments and in the relevance of the Commandments to contemporary life. It succeeded in emasculating the Commandments by interpreting each of them as divine ordinances embodying certain secular ethics. For example, the Commandment "Thou shalt not steal" in this version became a law of God concerning the "sanctity of private property." Overlooked utterly was the historic fact that the idea of private ownership of property is of comparatively recent novelty as well as the existential truth that the acquisition of property is *always* related to the dispossession of others. The latter is the case whether one is speaking of the ancient institutions of slavery in Israel's exile, or the subjection of the Greeks to the Romans, or the emergence of feudal estates and serfdom or, more lately, chattel slavery in the colonies and in the United States, or the neo-feudalism of European colonialism, or the apartheid regime in South Africa, or the more subtle deprivations wrought by *de facto* segregation and the increase of ghetto areas in modern American society.

This startling interpretation of the Eighth Commandment not only disregards history and the common experience of human beings, but it ruthlessly ignores the Biblical context of the gift of the Decalogue as the revelation of the fullness of the Word of God; moreover, it blithely omits mention of St. Paul's admonition that no man at any time is innocent of any of the Commandments, and, evidently, the authors of this manual have never even heard of the Letter of James (James 2:10).

If such tampering with the Word of God, as evidenced by this material, is taken, as it obviously is intended to be, as gospel by the laity to whom it is addressed, it authorizes them to oppose civil rights for Negro citizens, denounce free access to hotels and restaurants, refuse to sell or rent real estate on the basis of race, discriminate in hiring, firing, lending, merchandising, contracting and advertising, advocate suffrage conditioned on property ownership, sabotage the

war on poverty, seek the abolition of public welfare assistance and
argue against the graduated income tax on the grounds that all of
these policies are not only against their self-interests as propertied
people, but actually alien to the will of God.

Within the churches, this is a kind of pietism no less corrupting
than any pietism preoccupied with dancing or drinking or such. Significantly the former frequently accompanies the latter as the concrete
religious commitment of a particular person or class of people in
American Christendom.

Vulgar pietism, fascinated with the obviously (though never
merely) visceral functions, together with more esoteric pietism, like
that which distorts a Commandment to enhance a pagan property ethic,
do not exhaust the roster of indulgences to which Christians in America are vulnerable and to which they so often succumb. Some other
forms of pietism have been cited here before. There is the all too
familiar and peculiar pietism of which Norman Vincent Peale is the
prosperous merchant. Here individualistic ambitions are besought and
secured by hypnotic incantation, regardless of the costs or consequences
to other human beings. There are the dogmatic pietists — seminary
professors as well as "Sunday School" teachers are notorious among
them — whose pietism consists of threatening damnation to those who
conform not to what they say. There are many Anglicans, as well, no
doubt, as Roman Catholics, Lutherans and Orthodox, who are sometimes disposed to condescension toward Baptist or Methodist or Pres-
byterian brethren ensnared in more conventional pietism, who are
themselves no less pietistic in their regard for a supposed intrinsic
efficacy in mere ritual — who suppose that God's relationship with
His people is somehow jeopardized if the words are not invoked, or
the incense not flung, or the candles not lit, or the gongs not rung at
the prescribed times and in the ordained way.

In other words, though it be easy enough to ridicule the vulgar
pietists for their fascination with what they behold as lust, there are
many other kinds of pietism equally contemptible, just as superficial
and, probably, much more popularized. Virtually all churchmen in
America have been reared as pietists of one sort or another: that is
one reason why they are sometimes so ill-equipped in witness.

Yet, as there must be no pride in apostasy or heresy, there must
be none where churchmen treat the Gospel frivolously — as all pietists
do. After all, the earliest experiences of the Church encompassed all
of these things. For examples, St. Paul cautions against such pietism
when he opposes the "circumcision party" (Romans 2:25-29; Galatians 5:6), when he weighs the inheritance of the Law (Romans
2:12-24; I Corinthians 9:19-23), when he speaks of manners and
customs in the congregation (Galatians 5:16-24; Romans 1:28-32),
when he admonishes Christians about their conduct in the world outside the congregation (Romans 13:8-10; Colossians 2:8-19), when
he advises the early churches (Romans 14:1-9; Ephesians 5:3-20),
when he disciplines the churches (I Corinthians 8:4-13; Colossians
2:20-23), when he teaches that, by the virtue of Christ, all things
are lawful, though not always helpful (I Corinthians 6:12; 10:23).

For Paul, the bondage to pietism is equivocation toward God's
grace. For him, all pietism is "indulgence in the flesh," whether it be
in the form of gluttony or "positive thinking," drunkenness or com-
pulsive abstinence, sexual wantonness or the intellectual dissipation of
pedantic theologizing, larceny or the contradiction of a Commandment
in order to rationalize greed, common vice or superstitious ritualism.
For Paul, all these, and any of their counterparts, are abuses of grace,
all are indulgences in the flesh, all are futile and pathetic desires that
end in death.

The Letter of James does not quarrel with St. Paul in this respect
(James 1:14-15). Indulgence in the flesh means the aggrandizement
of human wants, ideas, pursuits, and enterprises despite the incapacity
of any of them to substitute for the work of Christ for all men, including all men who vainly strive in these ways. Indulgence in the flesh,
in any of its pietistic forms, though they be legion, always constitutes
the ultimate human frivolity because it represents the worship of death.

The Temptations of Christ

Specific temptations of all sorts — visceral, intellectual, psychical
— only mask the singular and ultimate temptation in which the power

of death poses as God. In that respect the Faustus legend, told and
retold, as it has been in so many ways, is a parable of the truth of
human existence in this world, and not just a quaint old fable. The
dignity and durability of the Faustus tale is in its portrayal of the
ingenious determination with which death beleaguers every man to
escape being haunted by the Word of God by worshipping death
instead of God.

That the *only* temptation at all, for any man, at any time, is to
succumb to the idolatry of death is disclosed and enacted decisively in
the episode of Jesus in the wilderness (Matthew 4:1-11; cf. Mark
1:2-13; Luke 4:1-13). Contrary to many "Sunday School" recitations,
the wilderness is not a period in which Jesus withdraws from the hurry
and hurly-burly of the cares and affairs of the world in order to escape
for awhile, practice asceticism, or meditate about the universe. Jesus
Christ in the wilderness, so to speak, is not like Ronald Coleman in
Shangri-La serenely pondering the ultimate. Nor is it, as the so-called
adoptionists (who are, secretly, very numerous in the churches) would
have it, an occasion in which Jesus finally stops procrastinating about
His own office and vocation. Jesus — in the wilderness any more than
in Gethsemane — doesn't resemble as it were, Adlai Stevenson agon-
izing about whether to accept a nomination.

The wilderness experience, first of all, evidences Jesus' remarkable identification with the generic ministry and mission of Israel,
recalling and recreating Israel's sojourn in the wilderness in intercession for all mankind.

Moreover, the wilderness interlude sums up the aggressiveness
with which death pursues Jesus from His conception and anticipates
death's relentlessness toward Him during His entire earthly ministry
— in His exercise of authority over the demonic in healing, in His
transcendence of time by renouncing the political ambitions that His
disciples covet for Him, in His rejection at the hands of His own
people, in His confounding of the ecclesiastical and imperial rulers
when they seize Him and scourge Him, in His submission to the last
vengeance of death on the Cross and in His victory over that
humiliation.

It is in such a context — not as some yoga or mystic or magician, not as a novice about the character of temptation — that Jesus is visited and tempted by the power of death in the wilderness.

It is written that Jesus in the wilderness had fasted for some time and was hungry; in the first assault of death upon Him is the challenge to turn stones into bread. The response of Jesus is that men live by the utterance of the Word of God, not only bread. (Though, let it be remembered, they do need bread.) The temptation is not so much an exploitation of a vulnerable circumstance — hunger — or even to demonstrate extraordinary powers — as it is the temptation to ridicule the Word of God as the source and substance of life itself and to renounce the Word of God not only in His own name but for all human beings and for the whole world (Matthew 4:1-4).

The power of death is not quickly daunted, and next is Jesus tempted to cast Himself from the pinnacle of the temple to prove His identity in the Word of God. His answer is to admonish the Devil not to tempt God. It seems, on the part of Jesus, an act of radical compassion to so disarm the assault of death by confessing His integrity in the Word of God and to thereby foretell the intercession for all mankind of God in Him on the cross (Matthew 4:5-7).

By now, it appears, chagrined, the Devil volunteers his own dominion to Jesus Christ — the kingdoms of this world — if only Jesus will acknowledge death as god. And in reply Jesus banishes the power of death and so heralds the Resurrection (Matthew 4:8-11).

In every instance in the wilderness episode, the confrontation is between the Devil and Jesus; in each it is exposed that the issue lies between the power of death and the Word of God which means life in the sense of men and God reconciled and, hence, the reconciliation of men within themselves, among one another, and to all things.

Christ's Intercessions for the Tempted

The wilderness encounter does not exhaust death's genius in temptation. Just as the power of death pursues Christ from the instant of His birth — when Herod sought to locate the infant Jesus in order to assassinate Him — so death besieges Christ throughout His ministry unto the Tomb. In truth, it is as if Easter is not some abrupt, startling, out-of-place occurrence, but quite the contrary, simply the consummation and epitomization of the drama of death and resurrection: of the aggressions of death defeated, of the extraordinary power of death but the even more awesome overpowering of death, of the versatile guises of death and of the ubiquity of God exposing each and all of them, of the assaults of death at once turned back and transcended in men's behalf.

The marvel of Easter, the glory of this day and event beyond that of any other in all history, is not that it is a unique, disjunctive, miraculous, incredible or spooky happening, but, rather, that it is definitively historic, wholly credible, typical and predictable, what is or should have been expected exactly, as the fulfillment and fruition of Christ's historical existence and His reiterated victorious confrontations with the power of death. That is why Easter has veracity as the authentic cosmic event.

Consider, for example, the intercession of Christ for mankind in the first utterance of the Lord's Prayer. Matthew 6 precedes the Prayer with a recitation of Jesus' caution against the emptiness of the public display of pietism (Matthew 6:1-9; cf. Luke 18:9-14). In the instruction and example of the Lord's Prayer, prayer has no intrinsic efficacy attaching to its performance, nor does it have to do with the desires of men; prayer has to do with the actual needs of men and the efficacy of prayer attaches to how God addresses those needs. Thus, Jesus admonishes, do not be religious, like those who "think that they will be heard for their many words . . . for your Father knows what you need before you ask Him" (Matthew 6:7b-8). That is Jesus' own introit to the Lord's Prayer. The summation of the Prayer is "lead us not into temptation, but deliver us from evil," that is "from the evil one," which is the power of death (Matthew 6:13). Evil does not, in the context of the Lord's Prayer, mean moral evil in its conventional definition and usage but refers to that which is evil for every man and for the whole of creation and that which is in fact secreted in every thought or deed or wish or word called evil: the power of death or, if one renders the proper name, the Devil.

I am aware how medieval it sounds to some contemporaries to speak of the Devil, though it is Biblical to do so, and though that which was medieval is not, by that mere token, untrue or inappropriate in the present time.* At the same time I am not, in using the term, thinking of some grotesque, supernatural, anthropomorphic being as such. I do not apprehend the Devil after the manner of those who conceive of God as a Santa Claus figure enthroned in the sky. Yet it does not offend my intellect or other sensibilities to invoke the name of the Devil to designate that power — distinguished *only* from God Himself — which is present and militant in this world in all relationships (e.g., work, sex, family, language, success, loneliness, indulgence) and to which all other powers (e.g., race, nation, religion, money, ideology, patriotism, athletics) are subjected. In a word it is the presumption of sovereignty over *all* of life that marks the power of death, and it is, as it were, the notorious vindication of that presumption over against everyone and everything else in this life in this world — apart *only* from God — that makes the employment of the name of the Devil, as unusual or archaic as it may nowadays seem, wholly apt and, so to speak, respectful of such an exceeding great power.

Manifestly, there are other ways in which the Lord's Prayer can be treated responsibly with respect to its origin, Biblical situation, and actual usage by Christian people, and, no doubt, as many ways again in which the same Prayer may be manipulated, abused or distorted, but neither of these issues alters or minimizes the intercession of Christ in the Lord's Prayer for a humanity in this world so gravely afflicted by the power of death.

That is verified by the further witness of the valor and consistency of Jesus own endurance of premonitions, preliminary attacks and other temptations upon His person, and by the power of death in His prayer for His bewildered disciples at Gethsemane. "I do not pray that thou shouldst take them out of the world, but that thou shouldst keep them from the evil one" (John 17:15). The work of Christ, exemplified in the very prayers of which He is author, and for which He is authority, and as it is embodied in the Cross and the

---

*A much more detailed discussion of this author's understanding of the meaning of death, as it relates to loneliness, sex, and work is found in *Instead of Death* (Seabury) and as it relates to ideologies and institutions in *Free in Obedience* (Seabury).

emancipation of Christ from the Tomb, is an intervention by God in this history for everyman in his particular suffering of the feigned, but ruthless, sovereignty of death over life.

Temptation, Sin and Death

The intercessions of Christ for the tempted represent the inexhaustible fidelity of God to men living under the threat of the power of death in this world. St. Paul comprehended this and proclaimed this assurance in his ministry as an apostle (II Thessalonians 3:3). It is the same confidence in the demonstration of God's faithfulness in Christ that authorizes James to say, "Let no one say when he is tempted, 'I am tempted by God'; for God cannot be tempted with evil and he himself tempts no one; but each person is tempted when he is lured and enticed by his own desire. Then desire when it has conceived gives birth to sin; and sin when it is full-grown brings forth death" (James 1:13-15).

Desire, it should not need to be again emphasized, does not have the connotation of simple lust, of visceral thoughts or acts alone, of carnal aggrandizement. Much more than that, desire means all sorts and forms of indulgence in the flesh, including those intellectual and physical and religious pietisms so popular in the churches in the present time. The crude language of James suits the practice of naming the power of death the Devil, for the image the Letter invokes is of the conception of sin in the confrontation of men with death in their temptations. In the metaphor implied in the Letter, the profound distortion of life, the alienation from the Word of God, the radical estrangement of men from themselves and one another and all things, which is sin, is born in the seduction and rape of men by the power of death — by the Devil.

Temptation is, thus, nothing so mundane or transient or simplistic as choosing "wrong" instead of "right," or surrendering to pleasure or pride, or being enticed by the ethics of self-interest: temptation refers rather, to the incitement men suffer to repudiate the gift of life by succumbing to the idolatry of death.

And sin, hence, does not mean that men are bad, or that men

have a proclivity for wickedness, or that they are proud and selfish, but, instead, sin is the possession of men by the power of death, the bondage and servitude of men to death, the usurpation of God's office by the arrogance of death. Sin does not mean that men are pernicious, it means that they are nihilists.

It is upon such a scene that God's faithfulness to men is manifested as not only the gift which it is in itself — a gift unearned by any merit or discretion, a gift without contingency or condition — but also as a gift that is justifying, a gift, as James gladly affirms, that surpasses and preempts each and all of death's temptations and substitutes and compensates for the eager affections of men for death (James 1:16, 17).

Temptation and Justification

Death has countless forms and faces. Death is hidden in everything that happens. The Devil is a genius of disguise. The power of death insinuates itself into every circumstance. Death commands legions of acolytes, many willful in their allegiance, but many, also, who are witless or unwary and who do not recognize death when actually confronting it.

Hence there are those who actually do not discern when they are being tempted by death and succumb to death's temptations for, so to speak, the most idealistic or earnest motives. In American Christendom, in the precincts of the familiar churches here, for all their divisions, competitions and other corruptions, it is typically this way. All varieties of pietism — moralistic, ritualistic and dogmatic — such as those mentioned earlier are evidences of the obtuseness of professed Christians to the versatility, subtlety, and ubiquity of death's temptations.

The pietists intend to say or think or do what is "right" for the sake of pleasing or appeasing or otherwise proving themselves before God. Pietists consistently have the purest intentions, but motives *never* determine or control the moral character of that which is committed in word or thought or deed. Pietism always consigns to God a merely collaborative role in the drama of salvation; pietism beholds

God as dependent and passive rather than free and active; pietism of all sorts seeks to make God a debtor of men; pietism discounts and, indeed, displaces God's unique prerogative as Judge of all things; pietism suffers the exceptional arrogance of professing to anticipate how God will judge each and every action and omission of men and nations.

In other words, pietism defiles the churches because of blindness to the power of death as the only tempter and to the concealment of death in every temptation. Pietism, whatever its particularity, embodies a lust for justification bereft of God. Pietism aspires to salvation without the benefit of God's life and action in this world, and thus always ends in death and in the idolatry of death.

Concretely, in the contemporary churches, pietism, in any of its forms, represents a profound anxiety for success, for results, for reputation, for tribute to the conduct, practices or beliefs of churchgoers. And though, characteristically, it is put to church people that they must behave, perform or believe in this way or that fashion for the approval or the pleasure of God, it is the world's recognition and applause that is coveted, while it remains the case, in fact, that all that is attained by such self-seeking is the contempt of the world for the church's conformity to the world's bondage to death. Pietism — to succumb to the temptation to pursue justification as if God had not already accomplished men's justification on His own initiative and in His own way — is pleasing only to the power of death.

The Joy of Trials

The absolution from pietism is that there is *no* way at all to please God, no way to strike a bargain with Him, no necessity to meet Him half-way, no way to detract from His sole office as Judge of all, no way in which His godliness can be diluted in dependency upon human enterprise. The futility of pietism, ending as it does in honoring death in the name of fidelity to God, is that God has triumphed over death already, in the here and now of this life. What is given to men, in that triumph, is not to add to God's achievement, since it is decisive, and it is not to complete His work, since God is not negligent, and much less is it to ridicule God's passion for this world by resort to moralistic legalism, mechanistic ritualism, doctrinaire meanness or any similar religious exercises. All that is given to men is to live now in God's triumph over death. What is given to men is to become and be, in the midst of all the wiles and temptations of the Devil, the immediate beneficiary of the Resurrection. What God has bestowed upon men is, indeed, as James puts it, "the crown of life" (James 1:12). That crown of life — that maturity of manhood in Christ — that fulfillment of life which is accredited exclusively to God's virtue — is not some far off destination, not some remote prize, not a reward for good talk or good works or good thoughts, but is a goal already reached, a victory long since won, a gift freely offered.

The vocation of men is to enjoy their emancipation from the power of death wrought by God's vitality in this world. The crown of life is the freedom to live now, for all the strife and ambiguity and travail, in the imminent transcendence of death, and all of death's threats and temptations. That is the gift of God to men in Christ's Resurrection.

Men of this vocation count all trials as joys, for, though every trial be an assault of the power of death, in every trial is God's defeat of death verified and manifested.

THE LETTER OF JAMES

CHAPTER 1

1 James, a servant of God and of the Lord Jesus Christ,
   To the twelve tribes in the dispersion:
   Greeting.

2 Count it all joy, my brethren, when you meet various trials,
3 for you know that the testing of your faith produces steadfastness.
4 And let steadfastness have its full effect, that you may be perfect and
complete, lacking in nothing.

5 If any of you lacks wisdom, let him ask God who gives to all
men generously and without reproaching, and it will be given him.
6 But let him ask in faith, with no doubting, for he who doubts is like
a wave of the sea that is driven and tossed by the wind. 7, 8 For that
person must not suppose that a double-minded man, unstable in all his
ways, will receive anything from the Lord.

9 Let the lowly brother boast in his exaltation, 10 and the rich
in his humiliation, because like the flower of the grass he will pass
away. 11 For the sun rises with its scorching heat and withers the
grass; its flower falls, and its beauty perishes. So will the rich man
fade away in the midst of his pursuits.

12 Blessed is the man who endures trial, for when he has stood
the test he will receive the crown of life which God has promised to
those who love him. 13 Let no one say when he is tempted, "I am

---

1. 10-11 : Is. 40. 6-7.

tempted by God"; for God cannot be tempted with evil and he him-self tempts no one; 14 but each person is tempted when he is lured and enticed by his own desire. 15 Then desire when it has conceived gives birth to sin; and sin when it is full-grown brings forth death.

16 Do not be deceived, my beloved brethren. 17 Every good endowment and every perfect gift is from above, coming down from the Father of lights with whom there is no variation or shadow due to change.*a* 18 Of his own will he brought us forth by the word of truth that we should be a kind of first fruits of his creatures.

19 Know this, my beloved brethren. Let every man be quick to hear, slow to speak, slow to anger, 20 for the anger of man does not work the righteousness of God. 21 Therefore put away all filthiness and rank growth of wickedness and receive with meekness the im-planted word, which is able to save your souls.

22 But be doers of the word, and not hearers only, deceiving yourselves. 23 For if any one is a hearer of the word and not a doer, he is like a man who observes his natural face in a mirror; 24 for he observes himself and goes away and at once forgets what he was like. 25 But he who looks into the perfect law, the law of liberty, and per-severes, being no hearer that forgets but a doer that acts, he shall be blessed in his doing.

26 If any one thinks he is religious, and does not bridle his tongue but deceives his heart, this man's religion is vain. 27 Religion that is pure and undefiled before God and the Father is this: to visit orphans and widows in their affliction, and to keep oneself unstained from the world.

CHAPTER 2

1 My brethren, show no partiality as you hold the faith of our Lord Jesus Christ, the Lord of glory. 2 For if a man with gold rings and in fine clothing comes into your assembly, and a poor man in shabby clothing also comes in, 3 and you pay attention to the one

---

a Some ancient authorities read *variation due to a shadow of turning.*

who wears the fine clothing and say, "Have a seat here, please," while you say to the poor man, "Stand there," or, "Sit at my feet," 4 have you not made distinctions among yourselves, and become judges with evil thoughts? 5 Listen, my beloved brethren. Has not God chosen those who are poor in the world to be rich in faith and heirs of the kingdom which he has promised to those who love him? 6 But you have dishonored the poor man. Is it not the rich who oppress you, is it not they who drag you into court? 7 Is it not they who blaspheme that honorable name by which you are called?

8 If you really fulfill the royal law, according to the scripture, "You shall love your neighbor as yourself," you do well. 9 But if you show partiality, you commit sin, and are convicted by the law as transgressors. 10 For whoever keeps the whole law but fails in one point has become guilty of all of it. 11 For he who said, "Do not commit adultery," said also, "Do not kill." If you do not commit adultery but do kill, you have become a transgressor of the law. 12 So speak and so act as those who are to be judged under the law of liberty. 13 For judgment is without mercy to one who has shown no mercy; mercy triumphs over judgment.

14 What does it profit, my brethren, if a man says he has faith but has not works? Can his faith save him? 15 If a brother or sister is ill-clad and in lack of daily food, 16 and one of you says to them, "Go in peace, be warmed and filled," without giving them the things needed for the body, what does it profit? 17 So faith by itself, if it has no works, is dead.

18 But some one will say, "You have faith and I have works." Show me your faith apart from your works, and I by my works will show you my faith. 19 You believe that God is one; you do well. Even the demons believe—and shudder. 20 Do you want to be shown, you foolish fellow, that faith apart from works is barren? 21 Was not Abraham our father justified by works, when he offered his son Isaac upon the altar? 22 You see that faith was active along with his works, and faith was completed by works, 23 and the scripture was fulfilled which says, "Abraham believed God, and it was reckoned

2. 8 : Lev. 19. 18.   2. 11 : Ex. 20. 13-14; Deut. 5. 17-18.
2. 21: Gen. 22. 1-14.   2. 23: Gen. 15. 6; Is. 41. 8; 2 Chr. 20. 7.

to him as righteousness''; and he was called the friend of God. 24 You see that a man is justified by works and not by faith alone. 25 And in the same way was not also Rahab the harlot justified by works when she received the messengers and sent them out another way? 26 For as the body apart from the spirit is dead, so faith apart from works is dead.

CHAPTER 3

1 Let not many of you become teachers, my brethren, for you know that we who teach shall be judged with greater strictness. 2 For we all make many mistakes, and if any one makes no mistakes in what he says he is a perfect man, able to bridle the whole body also. 3 If we put bits into the mouths of horses that they may obey us, we guide their whole bodies. 4 Look at the ships also; though they are so great and are driven by strong winds, they are guided by a very small rudder wherever the will of the pilot directs. 5 So the tongue is a little member and boasts of great things. How great a forest is set ablaze by a small fire!

6 And the tongue is a fire. The tongue is an unrighteous world among our members, staining the whole body, setting on fire the cycle of nature,[b] and set on fire by hell.[c] 7 For every kind of beast and bird, of reptile and sea creature, can be tamed and has been tamed by humankind, 8 but no human being can tame the tongue — a restless evil, full of deadly poison. 9 With it we bless the Lord and Father, and with it we curse men, who are made in the likeness of God. 10 From the same mouth come blessing and cursing. My brethren, this ought not to be so. 11 Does a spring pour forth from the same opening fresh water and brackish? 12 Can a fig tree, my brethren, yield olives, or a grapevine figs? No more can salt water yield fresh.

13 Who is wise and understanding among you? By his good life let him show his works in the meekness of wisdom. 14 But if you have bitter jealousy and selfish ambition in your hearts, do not

2. 25: Josh. 2. 1-21.
b Or *wheel of birth.*   c Greek *Gehenna.*

boast and be false to the truth. 15 This wisdom is not such as comes down from above, but is earthly, unspiritual, devilish. 16 For where jealousy and selfish ambition exist, there will be disorder and every vile practice. 17 But the wisdom from above is first pure, then peaceable, gentle, open to reason, full of mercy and good fruits, without uncertainty or insincerity. 18 And the harvest of righteousness is sown in peace by those who make peace.

CHAPTER 4

1 What causes wars, and what causes fightings among you? Is it not your passions that are at war in your members? 2 You desire and do not have; so you kill. And you covet[d] and cannot obtain; so you fight and wage war. You do not have, because you do not ask. 3 You ask and do not receive, because you ask wrongly, to spend it on your passions. 4 Unfaithful creatures! Do you not know that friendship with the world is enmity with God? Therefore whoever wishes to be a friend of the world makes himself an enemy of God. 5 Or do you suppose it is in vain that the scripture says, "He yearns jealously over the spirit which he has made to dwell in us?" 6 But he gives more grace; therefore it says, "God opposes the proud, but gives grace to the humble." 7 Submit yourselves therefore to God. Resist the devil and he will flee from you. 8 Draw near to God and he will draw near to you. Cleanse your hands, you sinners, and purify your hearts, you men of double mind. 9 Be wretched and mourn and weep. Let your laughter be turned to mourning and your joy to dejection. 10 Humble yourselves before the Lord and he will exalt you.

11 Do not speak evil against one another, brethren. He that speaks evil against a brother or judges his brother, speaks evil against the law and judges the law. But if you judge the law, you are not a doer of the law but a judge. 12 There is one lawgiver and judge, he who is able to save and to destroy. But who are you that you judge your neighbor?

13 Come now, you who say, "Today or tomorrow we will go into

---

d Or you kill and you covet.
4. 6 : Prov. 3. 34.

such and such a town and spend a year there and trade and get gain";
14 whereas you do not know about tomorrow. What is your life?
For you are a mist that appears for a little time and then vanishes.
15 Instead you ought to say, "If the Lord wills, we shall live and we
shall do this or that." 16 As it is, you boast in your arrogance. All
such boasting is evil. 17 Whoever knows what is right to do and fails
to do it, for him it is sin.

CHAPTER 5

1 Come now, you rich, weep and howl for the miseries that are
coming upon you. 2 Your riches have rotted and your garments are
moth-eaten. 3 Your gold and silver have rusted, and their rust will
be evidence against you and will eat your flesh like fire. You have
laid up treasure^c for the last days. 4 Behold, the wages of the laborers
who mowed your fields, which you kept back by fraud, cry out; and
the cries of the harvesters have reached the ears of the Lord of hosts.
5 You have lived on the earth in luxury and in pleasure; you have
fattened your hearts in a day of slaughter. 6 You have condemned,
you have killed the righteous man; he does not resist you.

7 Be patient, therefore, brethren, until the coming of the Lord.
Behold, the farmer waits for the precious fruit of the earth, being
patient over it until it receives the early and the late rain. 8 You also
be patient. Establish your hearts, for the coming of the Lord is at
hand. 9 Do not grumble, brethren, against one another, that you
may not be judged; behold, the Judge is standing at the doors. 10 As
an example of suffering and patience, brethren, take the prophets who
spoke in the name of the Lord. 11 Behold, we call those happy who
were steadfast. You have heard of the steadfastness of Job, and you
have seen the purpose of the Lord, how the Lord is compassionate
and merciful.

12 But above all, my brethren, do not swear, either by heaven
or by earth or with any other oath, but let your yes be yes and your
no be no, that you may not fall under condemnation.

---

^{c} Or *will eat your flesh, since you have stored up fire.*
5. 11: Job 1. 21-22; 2.10; Ps. 108. 8; 111. 4.   5. 12: Mt. 5. 37.

13 Is any one among you suffering? Let him pray. Is any cheerful? Let him sing praise. 14 Is any among you sick? Let him call for the elders of the church, and let them pray over him, anointing him with oil in the name of the Lord; 15 and the prayer of faith will save the sick man, and the Lord will raise him up; and if he has committed sins, he will be forgiven. 16 Therefore confess your sins to one another, and pray for one another, that you may be healed. The prayer of a righteous man has great power in its effects. 17 Elijah was a man of like nature with ourselves and he prayed fervently that it might not rain, and for three years and six months it did not rain on the earth. 18 Then he prayed again and the heaven gave rain, and the earth brought forth its fruit.

19 My brethren, if any one among you wanders from the truth and some one brings him back, 20 let him know that whoever brings back a sinner from the error of his way will save his soul from death and will cover a multitude of sins.

---

5. 17 : 1 Kings 17. 1; 18.1: Luke 4. 25.   5. 18 :   1 Kings 18. 42.